THE BBC TV SHAKESPEARE
Literary Consultant: John Wilders

THE WINTER'S TALE

THE BBC TV SHAKESPEARE

THE BBC TV SHAKESPEARE

Literary Consultant: John Wilders
Fellow of Worcester College, Oxford

The Winter's Tale

BRITISH BROADCASTING CORPORATION

Published by the
British Broadcasting Corporation
35 Marylebone High Street
London WiM 4AA

ISBN 0 563 17855 8

This edition first published 1981
© The British Broadcasting Corporation
and The Contributors 1981

The text of the Works of Shakespeare
edited by Peter Alexander
© William Collins Sons and Company Ltd 1951

The text of *The Winter's Tale* used in this volume is the Alexander text,
edited by the late Professor Alexander and chosen by the BBC as the basis
for its television production, and is reprinted by arrangement with William
Collins Sons and Company Ltd. The complete Alexander text is published
in one volume by William Collins Sons and Company Ltd under the title
The Alexander Text of the Complete Works of William Shakespeare

All photographs are BBC copyright (David Green)

Printed in England at
The Pitman Press, Bath

CONTENTS

PREFACE

John Wilders

The Winter's Tale is one of Shakespeare's plays for which we have a record of a very early performance. The astrologer Simon Forman recorded in his notebook that he went to a production of it at the Globe theatre in May 1611, and further evidence suggests that it was written earlier in the same year. It is one of the group of four plays, often known as the 'romances', which Shakespeare composed at the end of his career, of which the others are *Cymbeline*, *Pericles* and *The Tempest*. He adapted the story from *Pandosto or The Triumph of Time*, a very popular novel by Robert Greene, which was first published in 1588 and had been reprinted three times before the play was written.

All the earliest recorded performances, apart from the one attended by Simon Forman, were at the court and it has been thought to contain a hidden compliment to James I whose unification, on his accession to the throne, of the kingdoms of England and Scotland is paralleled by the union of the kingdoms of Sicilia and Bohemia by the marriage of Perdita to Florizel. A wholesale adaptation of *The Winter's Tale* by David Garrick, who gave it the new title *Florizel and Perdita*, replaced Shakespeare's play in the repertory at Drury Lane during the second half of the eighteenth century, and it was not until 1802 that John Philip Kemble produced a version which was more or less true to the original. In 1856 it was given a highly popular and spectacular production by Charles Kean and, in 1912, it was one of the plays which Granville Barker chose to present without cuts and on a simple platform stage. It was given in New York by the Theatre Guild in 1945 with Henry Daniell as Leontes and Eva Le Gallienne as Hermione; Peter Brook staged it in 1951 at the Phoenix Theatre, London, with John Gielgud and Diana Wynyard; and at Stratford, Ontario, in 1958 it was directed by Douglas Campbell with Christopher Plummer and Eileen Herlie. This television production by Jane Howell was recorded at the BBC Television Centre, London, in April 1980.

INTRODUCTION TO
THE WINTER'S TALE

John Wilders

As well as creating a wider range and variety of characters than any
other dramatist – from Iago and Falstaff to Rosalind and Lady
Macbeth – Shakespeare also portrayed a greater range of experiences. His characters fall in love, fight in battle, plot assassina-
tions, write poetry, govern kingdoms, put on plays, marry,
commit murder, get drunk and die. But the experience which
preoccupied him more consistently and frequently than any other
was the experience of time. There are many proverbs which
describe the effects of time, but the two most common of them
contradict each other: time is said to consume all things and it is
also said to be a great healer. The destructive power of time is the
subject of some of Shakespeare's greatest sonnets:

> When I have seen by Time's fell hand defaced
> The rich proud cost of outworn buried age;
> When sometime lofty towers I see down-rased,
> And brass eternal slave to mortal rage;
> When I have seen the hungry ocean gain
> Advantage on the kingdom of the shore,
> And the firm soil win of the wat'ry main,
> Increasing store with loss, and loss with store;
> When I have seen much interchange of state,
> Or state itself confounded to decay;
> Ruin hath taught me thus to ruminate –
> That Time will come and take my love away.

It is also one of the subjects of the two parts of *Henry IV*, in which,
as the Prince ripens towards the power he will inherit with the
throne, Falstaff and the King grow old and sicken towards death.
The healing effects of time, on the other hand, can be observed in
some of Shakespeare's comedies. It is time which, as Viola says,
'untangles the knot' of mistaken identities in *Twelfth Night*, and

time which brings together the various pairs of lovers at the end of *As You Like It*, a comedy which begins in 'winter and rough weather' and concludes in 'spring time, the only pretty ring time'.

The play which creates the strongest impression of the movement of time is, however, *The Winter's Tale*, a late work, written in about 1611, just before *The Tempest*. 'The Triumph of Time' was the subtitle of *Pandosto*, the prose romance, or novel, by Robert Greene from which Shakespeare took the outlines of the plot of this play, and into Greene's story he introduced the character of Time himself as a chorus. Time's opening words explain that his influence will be more complex than it has been in the sonnets or the comedies:

> I, that please some, try all, both joy and terror
> Of good and bad, that makes and unfolds error,
> Now take upon me, in the name of Time,
> To use my wings.

In *The Winter's Tale* Time is both creative and destructive: during the sixteen years which the action occupies, Perdita is born, she and Florizel fall in love, and eventually the family and friends are reunited, but during those same years Mamillius dies, Antigonus is killed, Leontes endures a period of solitude and penance, and wrinkles appear on the face of Hermione. The play embraces the contrary sensations of joy and terror, portrays both the good of Hermione's fidelity and the bad of Leontes' destructive paranoia, pleases some of the characters but 'tries' (or 'tests') all of them. It is neither a comedy nor a tragedy but a tragi-comedy, not only in the sense that its characters come to the very edge of disaster and are then allowed a reprieve, but also in the sense that its action encompasses both tragic and comic experiences: birth and death, youth and age, sophisticated court and simple country life, rustic dances and judicial trials, bears and pickpockets. It is probably Shakespeare's most inclusive play, the one which holds the most extensive mirror up to nature.

In the opening scenes, the characters are much preoccupied with memories of time past, especially Polixenes who fondly recalls his childhood friendship with Leontes and the innocence which they once shared but have subsequently lost:

> We were as twinn'd lambs that did frisk i'th' sun
> And bleat the one at th'other. What we chang'd
> Was innocence for innocence; we knew not

The doctrine of ill-doing, nor dream'd
That any did.

His wistful recollections of boyhood, which he compares to the freshness and vitality of spring, suggest that he would have preferred, had it been possible, never to have grown up. A similar nostalgia for pre-sexual innocence is expressed by Leontes, as he recognises in his son Mamillius his own childhood features, and bitterly contrasts the boy's harmless games with the furtive, loathsome sexual games in which he imagines his wife is indulging with Polixenes:

Go, play, boy, play; thy mother plays, and I
Play too; but so disgrac'd a part, whose issue
Will hiss me to my grave. Contempt and clamour
Will be my knell. Go, play, boy, play.

Whereas *The Winter's Tale* opens with a recollection of childhood which is associated, through Shakespeare's language, with the season of spring, the increasingly painful events which occupy most of the first section (up to the end of Act III) gradually become associated with winter, particularly when, following Hermione's apparent death, Paulina delivers to Leontes her terrible injuction:

Do not repent these things, for they are heavier
Than all thy woes can stir; therefore betake thee
To nothing but despair. A thousand knees
Ten thousand years together, naked, fasting,
Upon a barren mountain, and still winter
In storm perpetual, could not move the gods
To look that way thou wert.

Her description of the stormy winter landcape is followed shortly afterwards by an actual storm in the midst of which Antigonus arrives with the newly-born Perdita on the remote and barren shore of Bohemia. 'We have landed,' says one of the mariners,

in ill time; the skies look grimly
And threaten present blusters.

It is at this point – when Mamillius is already dead, Hermione has apparently died, Leontes has begun his long vigil of repentance, the infant has been exposed to the hazards of a wild, winter country, the ship has been wrecked and Antigonus devoured by the bear – that the play comes closest to tragedy. But what appears to be a tragic ending is in fact the beginning of a new movement away from tragedy. The link between the violent first section of the play and the pastoral second section is the child Perdita, placed on the earth by Antigonus and taken up again by the old shepherd, whose words to his son mark the division between the two sections and indicate what the difference between them will be: 'Thou met'st with things dying, I with things new-born.'

Although there is a break in the play at this point, after which the action is resumed sixteen years later, Shakespeare creates the impression that the winter during which the previous scenes have taken place is followed immediately by the spring, the season of 'things new-born'. Autolycus is its herald:

> When daffodils begin to peer,
>   With heigh! the doxy over the dale,
> Why, then comes in the sweet o'the year,
>   For the red blood reigns in the winter's pale.

By the next scene, however, it is clear that the year has advanced into high summer for, throughout the episode of the sheep-shearing feast, Shakespeare creates a rich visual and poetic impression of fruitfulness and plenty. On her first entrance, Perdita, who has now, like the year, come to maturity, seems to usher in the summer season itself, garlanded as she is with flowers:

> Here's flow'rs for you:
> Hot lavender, mints, savory, marjoram;
> The marigold, that goes to bed wi' th' sun,
> And with him rises weeping; these are the flow'rs
> Of middle summer, and I think they are given
> To men of middle age.

In their feast the rural folk celebrate and give thanks for their fellowship one with another and for the blessings of nature.

Although there is what Leontes calls a 'wide gap of time' between the first and second sections, Shakespeare associates the process of division and reunion within the family with the cycle of the seasons during a single year. By this means, the process in which the characters are engaged – from their initial, painful separation to their final, joyful reconciliation – is made to resemble the natural, seasonal process of destruction and recreation, death and resurrection. The seasonal references also connect the older characters, especially Leontes and Polixenes, with winter, and the younger characters, Florizel (whose name is derived from the Latin word meaning 'flower' or 'blossom') and Perdita, with spring. Indeed, on her return to Sicilia, Perdita is said to be as welcome 'as is the spring to th' earth'. The implication is that the difference between the generations parallels the difference between the seasons; man and nature are alike in that the new stock grows from the roots of the old, and the violence committed by the older generation is overcome by the innocence and optimism of the young. By connecting his characters with the natural landscape, Shakespeare also gives to the play the features of one of the myths evolved in antiquity as a way of accounting for the cycle of the seasons. One such myth was that of Proserpina (actually mentioned in Act IV Scene iv line 116), who was compelled to spend half the year confined to the internal regions of Hades, but on whose annual return to earth in the spring nature itself burst into life in sympathy with her arrival. *The Winter's Tale* can be seen as Shakespeare's version of such a myth in which the land of Sicilia suffers a period of darkness, sterility and mourning as a result of Leontes' violence, but is brought to life again by Perdita's return to her father's winter court.

As well as being a play about the passage and effects of time, *The Winter's Tale* is also, therefore, a play about nature, the repeated seasonal processes of which are analagous to the separation, reunion and revival of Leontes and his family. It is also a play which arouses in the minds of the audience a strong sense of nature of a different kind: the natural, instinctive affections which bind together husband and wife, parents and children, friend and friend, master and servant, man and the land where he is born. Throughout his work, Shakespeare shows a deep awareness of the bonds which hold together communities, especially the intimate communities of family and household. These bonds are often broken at the beginning of the tragedies: Lear banishes his daughter Cordelia and is, in turn, cast out by her sisters; Macbeth murders his kinsman and his guest, Duncan; and Hamlet sees in his mother's remarriage a betrayal of loyalty to his father. Moreover, most of his comedies end with the formation or re-establishment of links of this kind, as the lovers assemble for the ritual of marriage or, as in *As You Like It*, the Duke and his courtiers prepare to return home. *The Winter's Tale* begins with the breaking of the bonds which unite the family and, for this reason, its first section resembles the tragedies, but it ends with the re-establishment of these links in a way which resembles the endings of the comedies.

By attempting to murder his childhood friend, banishing his

newly-born daughter and falsely accusing his wife of adultery, Leontes behaves in a way which we recognise as violently 'unnatural'. The bonds which he has severed are described explicitly by Hermione in the speech she delivers in her defence, and, in defining them, she explains how necessary they are to give meaning and support to life:

> To me can life be no commodity.
> The crown and comfort of my life, your favour,
> I do give lost, for I do feel it gone,
> But know not how it went; my second joy
> And first fruits of my body, from his presence
> I am barr'd, like one infectious; my third comfort,
> Starr'd most unluckily, is from my breast –
> The innocent milk in it most innocent mouth –
> Hal'd out to murder; myself on every post
> Proclaim'd a strumpet; with immodest hatred
> The child-bed privilege denied, which 'longs
> To women of all fashion; lastly, hurried
> Here to this place, i'th' open air, before
> I have got strength of limit. Now, my liege,
> Tell me what blessings I have here alive
> That I should fear to die.

Her words, while providing a summary of the action up to this point, express in feelingly personal terms how essential are the relationships of which she speaks, and with what monstrous inhumanity her husband has destroyed them. It is only when he himself believes that he has lost her irrecoverably that he, in turn, discovers how necessary she was to him as the object of his love.

Whereas the first section of *The Winter's Tale* portrays the painful fragmentation of a family, the second section shows us a community united in the celebration of its companionship. The interdependence of the rural folk of Bohemia is expressed by the communal occupations of singing, dancing and feasting in which they participate. Their genial sense of hospitality is also conveyed in the old shepherd's recollections of the time when his wife was mistress of the feast:

> When my old wife liv'd, upon
> This day she was both pantler, butler, cook;
> Both dame and servant; welcom'd all; serv'd all;
> Would sing her song and dance her turn; now here
> At upper end o'th' table, now i'th' middle;

On his shoulder, and his; her face o'fire
With labour, and the thing she took to quench it
She would to each one sip.

The sheep-shearing festival is like a rural scene painted by
Brueghel. It expresses a spontaneous delight in the companionship
which exists between neighbour and neighbour, old and young,
hostess and guests, the labourers and the soil on which they
depend and whose fruitfulness depends on them. But, like
Brueghel's rustics, Shakespeare's country people are not idealised
or sentimentalised. For all their good humour, they are coarse,
slow-witted and easily deceived. Their simplicity allows Autolycus
to cheat and profit from them and, as he does so, we recognise
their limitations.

The gradual reassembly in the last act of the domestic group we
glimpsed very briefly at the beginning of the first act is also
brought about by the inherent, natural needs of the characters.
The instigator of the return to Sicilia is Camillo who longs to

Purchase the sight again of dear Sicilia
And that unhappy king, my master, whom
I so much thirst to see.

But it is also the irresistible love of Florizel for Perdita which
drives them, together, from his father's wrath and, under Camillo's guidance, steers them back to Leontes' court. As the love of
Leontes for the supposedly dead Hermione makes him confine
himself to his long period of mourning and remorse, so the love of
Florizel for Perdita impels him to defy his father, risk the loss of
his succession to the crown, and take flight to Sicilia:

Not for Bohemia, nor the pomp that may
Be thereat glean'd, for all the sun sees or
The close earth wombs, or the profound seas hides
In unknown fathoms, will I break my oath
To this my fair belov'd.

It is not mere chance which brings family and friends together but
the desire to satisfy natural and irresistible needs, and it is the
apparently miraculous fulfilment of those needs which makes the
final moments of the play – the reunion of Hermione with her
daughter and husband – so deeply moving.

The resurrection of Hermione is the most radical change which
Shakespeare made to Robert Greene's story. In *Pandosto* the queen
dies of grief and never revives. To Shakespeare's first audiences,

some of whom may have known Greene's story (for it was a popular work and had been reprinted many times), the statue scene must have been astonishing. To modern audiences unfamiliar with *Pandosto* it is still highly dramatic, largely because of the care with which Shakespeare prepares the way for it. Our last sight of Leontes as he begins his long vigil is of a man deeply bereaved, and when, sixteen years later, he reappears he is still totally possessed by feelings of guilt and loss:

> Whilst I remember
> Her and her virtues, I cannot forget
> My blemishes in them, and so still think of
> The wrong I did myself; which was so much
> That heirless it hath made my kingdom, and
> Destroy'd the sweet'st companion that e'er man
> Bred his hopes out of.

In Leontes we observe a man who thirsts for the reconciliation which neither he nor we can yet hope for. Moreover, in order not to diminish the dramatic power of the final scene, Shakespeare allows the revelation of Perdita's identity and the reunion of Leontes with Polixenes to take place off stage, and it is in the aftermath of the excited account, by the three courtiers, of their meeting that we come to the climactic episode. Even then the moment of reconciliation is delayed and, when Paulina draws back the curtain to reveal the statue, Leontes responds with an astonished silence. The sense of awe and expectation increases as Paulina calls for music and the statue begins to breathe human life:

> Music, awake her; strike.
> 'Tis time; be stone no more; approach;
> Strike all that look upon with marvel. Come;
> I'll fill your grave up. Stir; nay, come away.
> Bequeath to death your numbness, for from him
> Dear life redeems you.

The moment derives its power from the care with which Shakespeare has gradually led us up to it and holds both the characters and audience in prolonged suspense before the apparent miracle occurs. He arouses our expectations, sustains them, fulfils them and then surpasses them.

Yet in the final lines of the play, the dramatist makes us as much aware of what has been lost as what has been restored. The dead Mamillius will never return, Paulina resoves to mourn for her 'mate, that's never to be found again', and the signs of age on Hermione's face are evidence of the wasted years of what could have been love and companionship. Time, which pleases some, tries all.

THE PRODUCTION

Henry Fenwick

Jane Howell is unusual in the run of Shakespeare directors so far, not least because she is a woman and women directors are still distressingly few on the ground in television. She is unusual, too, in appearing, to my eye at least, much more intense in her approach than any of the previous directors. (This is not to say that they were casual!) She worries openly, continually; even her jokes are fundamentally serious.

Jonathan Miller, reluctant at first to say in what way his directors differed, preferred to emphasise the ways in which they resembled each other. 'What I looked for in them all was vigour, common sense, lack of sentimentality, a modernity without gimmickry, a muscular vigour of imagination.' Pressed to characterise each one further, he finally added to those qualities in her the observation that she was 'interestingly puritanical'. I think I know what he means. She is a no-nonsense figure who seems unseduceable by the usual frou-frous of theatricality and showbusiness. Some people described her to me as an intellectual, but that, I think, is a misleading term. Miller himself may be an intellectual, with an awesome body of scholarship behind him. Jane Howell operates rather on an intensity of attention: when she talks she does so gropingly, as though feeling her way by instinct, with no easy flow of words.

She herself gruffly laughs off the imputation: 'Me? Intellectual? Good God! I keep getting accused of this. I deny it!' Her assistant demurs slightly from such a swingeing denial: 'You do seem to know exhaustively the background of everything you're doing.' 'Well,' she finally allows, 'I do like covering my tracks.' Covering her tracks means doing months of homework before starting a production: when she was directing *The Dybuck* for the BBC she says she sat on her sofa every night for about two and a half months reading Jewish theology. Such homework, she says, is especially necessary since she learned nothing at school. 'It was all so *boring*! But you need to know for plays – the theatre has educated me.'

The Winter's Tale is a play she has already directed twice before on stage, and it is, not surprisingly, close to her. 'The first production was when I must have been twentyish and a friend of mine called Douglas Livingstone – Doug's a very good telly writer now – and I put on an amateur production in the Irving Theatre, Leicester Square, which was also a strip theatre. We did *Winter's Tale* first, then the strippers would come in after, through the roof of the dressing-room from the Chinese restaurant next door. We used to start at about seven, and they didn't start till about half past ten.' The couple, full of chutzpah, wrote to all the critics and a great number came, including Harold Hobson, who was fired with one of his well-known enthusiasms and said it was the best spoken verse he'd ever heard. 'It was wonderful – we were just kids.'

The next production, ten years later, was less wonderful. 'I was working with actors I didn't know and I'm always unhappy then. It didn't really count, the production – it was competent but it wasn't from the middle of me.' Another ten years later ('extraordinary, my ten-year play, at very different stages of my life!'), this particular production means a lot to her, she says. 'That's why I get upset! Because it's never perfect! Is it? It's never *right*.' She parodies her own worrying tone, in self-mockery.

It is, I suggest, a particularly difficult play for television – the sudden swift changes of mood, the bizarre plot, the notes of myth and magic, all seem more suited to the stage. She demurs: 'I don't think television is realistic – I don't think it needs to be. What needs to be – what has got to be real – is the actor's performance, but what's around that need not be realistic at all.' She feels no qualms in frankly following the stage conventions of production. 'I believe that plays have rules. When I did *St Joan* on television I was very aware for example of how Shaw had imagined St Joan should be done. It's the same with Shakespeare. I think it's terribly important with any classic play that you understand the original rules under which it was performed. You have to know both the social history and the physical shape of the theatre, because I think you break those rules at your peril. Simple things like the fact that there are two entrances; that there is an upper stage – though in *Winter's Tale* that doesn't apply, it's not used at all – that the actors play standing up, basically, unless he mentions that there's a seat. I'm not suggesting in any way that Shakespeare plays should be done on Elizabethan stages, but there is something about the fact that you have an entrance and an exit – the *speed* at which scenes follow on, probably starting and ending scenes with the opening and shutting of doors at the back – you're down at the front, you finish a scene and as the last line is spoken the door opens, this lot is dismissed, and as the old lot shut the door the new lot start: that I suspect is the rhythmic sensation of the play. That seemed important to preserve and that was what I talked an awful lot to Don [Don Homfray, the set designer] about. I said, "We've got to preserve the rules of the play: the actors have got to play standing up for the main part, in order to provide the correct energy." That automatically is going to lead you to a stylised solution.

'The Winter's Tale has the sensation of being a fairy story. It is very strange; it is obviously based on Elizabethan life: Bohemia and Sicily are, as someone suggested, more like Wandsworth and Warwickshire, it's so rooted in England; but at the same time the characters mention things like Apollo. They obviously just mean God, but it does put a distance on it.

'I did go through the play almost naturalistically at one point, and did a lot of work – I planned scenes in bedrooms and scenes in very dark corridors; and if I'd been filming abroad in an old wooden palace in Rumania it would have been a very different show. But I wasn't, I was in the television studio. Also I am interested in breaking away from naturalism – whatever that word means! I suppose it comes from being seventeen years in the theatre, but I'm more interested in an essence than in "reality" – I get very *bored* with "reality"!

'Another thing that seemed to me to be important was the sense of the seasons. Every director finds his own starting place in it and I was brought up in the country, then when I was nine I came to London. I was literally educated by the trees and the grass until that point, I think; then I came to London and started reading books. And I do believe in the value of both those things. The character of Perdita interests me very much because it seems she has the graces of both ways of being brought up: she has the simplicity and honesty of the country and she also has a true sophistication of the town and education inbred in her. She and Hermione are the most balanced people in the play and it seems a play about balance, and about reconciliation. And – as in all good pantomimes! – the seasonal sense has always seemed to me to be very important. That's why I started in winter, which seems to be a time when the emotions are vulnerable anyway, and it's cold and it's a time of little growth, then it goes right through the seasons to spring again, to new growth, new learning.'

Wasn't that sense of seasonal change a particularly difficult thing to accomplish in the studio, I ask. 'No, I don't think seasons are difficult to represent in the studio at all. In *The Dybuck* we had to do the wastes of Rumania or whatever, so TC1 [the studio] was white and it looked as though it went on for ever. I didn't want a space which went on for ever in this play, I wanted a limited space: winter is white and there is one tree and it's bare; in the country scene it is still there but it has its autumn leaves on and the spaces which were white before are now golden – it might be corn, it might be stripped fields, anything you might want. That's another important thing, to leave space for people's minds. That's why I think I hate the four-square limitations of "reality": when I look at it there is no space for my mind to add. It's also very dangerous in Shakespeare to show everything, because the words are telling you so much. I remember, as a very young director, doing a play by Fry; the set had a big window at the back and there was a bloke talking about the sunset and I was trying, in lighting terms, to show the sunset through this window at the back. Then at dress rehearsal I realised suddenly that this was very foolish; you either rely on the words or show it, never both. That rule, I think, applies to Shakespeare: you have to be very careful what you show, you have to be very selective.

'Another central thing, I think, comes in something Perdita says after Polixenes has been terribly cross with her and gone stalking off. She says:

I was about to speak and tell him plainly
The self-same sun that shines upon his court
Hides not his visage from our cottage here, but
Looks on alike . . .

The world is a unity, it is a very small place – and what seemed to me important from that (I don't know where these things come from, but they do) is that whatever the basic set was, it had to be the same for the country and for the court. It had to be the same space, only looked at, as it were, through a different lens. It might be a different colour but it was the same place and it depended on what was in your head. I kept saying to Don, "All I can see, dear, I'm very sorry, is a white page and a yellow page and a black page with these people on it, like illustrations for a children's book."'

'We went through the whole play,' says Homfray, 'and Jane had these very strong images: about light and darkness, about corridors and diminishing perspectives and a feeling of choice – we talked about intersecting corridors: there are two paths, you could go down one, you could go down the other. She also wanted a tree – she was very strong about that. She saw a tree that was dead and that came to life, rather like *Waiting for Godot*, and we distanced it from being a real tree by painting it.

'Jane felt that one of the themes of the play is that life is always the same and that it depends on how you open yourself to it, what you do to it, that makes you see it differently. The landscape of life, if you like, is seen in a certain way; but if a different action is taken, a different choice is made, then the landscape changes. So we felt that the set should always be the same place but always seen slightly differently; there would be a dark area where one saw nothing but people in darkness, and an area where it was very bright and one was in a landscape which changed according to what actually happened. Then in the last shots of the play we linked the two areas up with a camera pan right across, taking the play out of the dark area into the light.'

The actual physical construction of the set – a flat area surrounded by wedge-shaped ramps with exits and entrances cut through them – was for Homfray a development, an extension of the work he had already done for Cedric Messina's *Henry V* and *Hamlet*. 'We decided we didn't want any illusion. In *Henry V* I got trapped between illusion and non-illusion. It's very easy to make illusions and it isn't necessarily the right thing to do. We wanted the pictures to be beautiful, in some instances, and harsh and hard but *not real*, not illusionistic. You were always in the same space, which wasn't a real landscape and wasn't an interior, just a space with shapes. The ramps around the space we decided we weren't going to use for anybody to go on this time; they were merely going to be a three-dimensional background which you could change the surface of. The ramps finished up in these funny wedge shapes because it gave a diminishing perspective, which is what we wanted. We could also change the colours on the sloping surface – white, then gold, then green at last. There wasn't a sky, just colours on the cyc., with no attempt at directional lighting or imitating a sky, no attempt at making cloud formations or anything like that. For the storm the sky just went very dark and louring, then yellow for the country scene. We were using light like a paintbrush, rather like kids' paintings.'

The stylisation applied to the costumes as well as to the sets. As designer John Peacock points out, the play can be set in any period. 'Jane didn't particularly want any period; she knew the *feel* that she wanted, she knew the colours she wanted and she knew the sort of fabrics she wanted me to use – it came down to wools and furs – and she wanted costumes that might be detailed close up but from a distance looked like set shapes. It became a matter of working with, say, grey-green on grey-green, so that in close-up the detail shows but from a distance you can't see it. Jane and I talked through the play and the way she felt in terms of paintings, and her references really did range from Botticelli to Bruegel to van Eyck – as far apart as that. It was really atmosphere she was talking about.

'Then we had another meeting to talk specifically about characters. Leontes at the beginning of the play is big and overpowering and unbending, while Polixenes is romantic and loving and fits in with Hermione far better than Leontes seems to. As the play progresses Jane wanted them to change places, so I started Leontes in heavy furs and Polixenes in light colours, but by the end of the play Polixenes is in very dark heavy robes with lots of fur on them and Leontes is in a light-coloured robe with not so much fur, which makes him look younger. I tried to do the same thing with Hermoine, who starts off as a pretty, fragile pregnant lady, goes through to the prison scene where she's drained and ill and can't cope with what's happened to her, and then we see her as a fragile piece of sculpture.'

Disguising a real woman as a piece of sculpture 'we just dressed the actress all in white, concealing everything of the body that we could apart from the hand outstretched. We covered the hair completely. I used heavy fabric so it fell in folds that it would have been possible to have sculpted. I tried to see round the whole thing to see what it was possible to chip out of marble. And I think it worked – Anna Calder-Marshall did come to life!

'The period I suppose I dressed the play in was early 1600s, but it went backwards and forwards quite a bit, so it's impossible to say any specific period. Perdita was pure Botticelli – or I tried to make her look pure Botticelli. The peasants were Bruegel – a different period altogether from the rest! The most magical scenes were the country scenes: Autolycus, for instance, we see first when he throws himself in front of the clown as though he's been robbed. I had the idea that he had a magic coat that he took off and turned inside out and it was rags. The same with his hat: he could pull it into a certain position and it would look as though it had been really battered. Then this idea developed. When we see him change clothes with Florizel, Florizel has a magic coat as well – a shepherd's coat when he is wearing it at first, turned inside out it turns into a grand gentleman's coat. He also turns the shepherd's hat inside out and it's all embroidered and pretty inside. It was fun to do.'

Whenever *The Winter's Tale* is mounted, the stage direction 'Exit pursued by a bear' is a classic difficulty for any director. 'It still is a classic difficulty,' Jane Howell grins when I ask her about it. 'I was desperate for a real bear but the problems of getting one from Chipperfield's and a man with a gun and a short lead in TC1 and the expense! I presume Shakespeare did have a real bear – they had a bear pit next door so he sent over to his mate and said "Bring Bruno in this afternoon at three o'clock and let him chase so and so". In my other productions I've always used the bear as a comic shunt in the play, to say, "All right, from here on in, lads, we're going to have a few laughs." On the stage I don't see how you can not do that. But thinking about it this time I became obsessed by the idea that in a strange way the bear is the long arm of Leontes – there is an inevitable outcome to a wrong action, and even after your particular wave has passed (because Leontes has said he's sorry by this time) it will still ricochet on round the world and cause trouble. I don't suppose anyone will notice, but gradually in the first half Leontes does wear more and more fur and by the trail scene he looks more debased and animal-like. I've tried to give the bear some power. You don't actually see him following Antigonus, he comes towards the camera and as he does everything goes into blackness and then it mixes through into the same set – it's still the beach – but much gentler colours, and the shepherd is sitting there, and the play as it were turns over and starts coming up the other way.'

Casting for Jane is a long and arduous process – she is probably above all a director who relies on her actors and needs to work closely with them: 'There's a rapport thing. If I had someone in the room whom I can't do that to [she stretches over and pats my leg] I can't work. I cannot work! I can't work on dissension – a lot of directors do and deliberately seek it out and work on friction; I can't work that way, I have to work on affection and if that is blocked I can't speak, I can't do anything. I get neurotic, boring, *difficult!*' She naturally tends, therefore, to work with people again and again. In this case the central piece of casting was Jeremy Kemp as Leontes. 'I cast Jeremy first and built everything to him,' she says. 'He was wonderful as Warwick in *Saint Joan* and I wanted to see him in a big leading part taking responsibility for a

23

play.' Other cast members she had previously worked with were David Burke as Camillo, 'and there were three in the country scene – Mopsa, Dorcas and the clown who had been in my company at Exeter. I hadn't worked with them since, which was five years ago. Suddenly to work with them again was wonderful – so much work had already been done: they'd been with me for three years.'

It was the spiritual qualities of the women she found particularly hard to cast. Anna Calder-Marshall, who plays Hermione, Jane had known for some time (she is married to David Burke), but they had never worked together. 'I didn't want Hermione to be a statuesque English blonde; I wanted her to be someone. You know when you meet people and you mistake them first of all, you enjoy their company and you find them fun but you don't think any more about them, then as you get to know them you realise they've actually got backbones of steel – I don't mean in an unpleasant sense, I mean in deep moral values. For me Anna is one of those women. But she is *tiny*! Then we had to find an even smaller Perdita! In rehearsal I could stand with those two tucked under either arm! I got very neurotic about casting Florizel and Perdita – the quality of innocence is so important. We decided they had to be very young and in the end these two kids read together and caught my heart and I thought they would catch Jeremy's too.'

She decided against stressing the sixteen-year gap in the plot when it came to ageing the actors: 'I haven't pushed the ageing at all. I think in sixteen years when you're between thirty and the late forties you don't age very much anyway, and I didn't want to take it into the sere and yellow. Also, it did seem important that there should be a sexual possibility at the end with Hermione – that the whole thing should be handed back to him.'

The plot of *The Winter's Tale*, with its abrupt passions, far-flung coincidences and miraculous ending, makes special demands on us today. 'I suspect it's less difficult for the audience than it is for the actors,' says Howell. 'A friend of mine said it doesn't really matter which actor says the lines in a Shakespeare play because the story will come over anyway. Now you can't actually say that to the actors but it is true that the story is more important than they are. They are at the service of the story. But how you cajole that out of them without telling them that is a different matter. You have to lay in some sort of psychological basis – but it's for the actors, not for the audience. The audience see the sudden start and they know why it's happening, that's all. Leontes' sudden jealousy is very abrupt but I understand it in the sense that it's one of those irrational things we all do at times – you look at two people you love and for some reason they suddenly look like a couple. It's like the Snow Queen story: a piece of ice has gone into your eye and you're suddenly seeing things differently, your perceptions are thrown, and from a small germ you grow a tree of horror and people die. I think the evil of the world *is* that irrational.'

For both Hermione and Leontes this sudden irrational jealousy and anger pose major acting problems. For Anna Calder-Marshall one of the difficulties, she felt, was that in the lines there is no chance to see the relationship between Leontes and Hermione before the jealousy. What, therefore, she tried to get and hold on to for as long as possible in the initial scene was the sense of a happy marriage, a family, 'and my not being able to understand what was happening until quite late on'. Though her real-life husband, David Burke, was playing Camillo, not Leontes, nevertheless they worked together on her scenes at home. 'I remember,' says David, 'for a long time that was a very difficult scene to get into. What do you do if after years of being happily married to a man he suddenly comes home one night and starts calling you a whore, in front of the whole court!'

'I said to David,' Anna remembers, ' "Could *you* say it to me?" I kept wondering what would I think! Then one night he actually did it at home and I was able to sort it out. Sometimes acting is tapping your own reality – it can unlock part of yourself if you get stuck.'

'I think in the last group of plays Shakespeare was getting impatient with the mechanics of plot and he wanted to get launched into this story of a jealous man, so he thought, "Let's get on with it," ' says Jeremy Kemp. 'It does make quite a demand on the actor. He comes on and says, "Darling, how are you?", and everything's all right, and then by the end of the scene he's' – and he opens his mouth in a demonstrating roar of leonine fury. 'I took the view that whatever had been festering in somebody's mind, there has to be one definite and explicit moment when it all comes together, and I tried to suggest that the temperament of his wife is such that it could be misinterpreted and that Leontes was not a very secure chap. You have to remember that he comes out of it just as suddenly – and *that* perhaps is a greater problem for an actor than getting into it. He denies faith in the oracle, then his son dies, the queen collapses, Paulina comes in and calls him all kinds of things, and he takes it all in and stands up to it: it's a huge thing to encompass. You have to call on more emotional reserves and strength to take in those things and behave accordingly.'

It was the final scene, however, which he felt was most difficult of all. 'Among other things the play is about forgiveness: Jane's phrase, I remember, was being given a second chance – Leontes is given a second chance. He himself is, in a manner of speaking, brought back from stone. You see him in Act 5 being warmed up by the children and, if he were grey, salmon-colour would gradually work up and up till he ended human pink instead of grey old granite. That pianissimo is more difficult to bring off success-fully than a big forte passage – or as difficult. And there's nothing in the rule book about how you should behave. Particularly with the statue coming to life. The long-lost child is perhaps easier, one could perhaps call on experiences, but if you were driving through Parliament Square and the statue of Winston Churchill gradually began to take on life you really wouldn't know quite what to do about it! I think it's largely a matter of deciding how dead Hermione is to Leontes. I think in physician's terms he believes her quite dead but, as he led this austere life because of what had occurred and because he was constantly reminded of her by Paulina, she was still very much alive in his head. From that notion I tried to suggest that it was not so utterly improbable as one would imagine. And purely technically there is quite a contribution the actress can make, in that slow growth from something which is self-evidently not human into dear old Dot. Anna's contribution was very strong and helpful. The moment of realisation became the moment she elected to recognise me.'

The experience of playing the statue who comes to life was, Anna Calder-Marshall found out, disturbing. 'Being totally still with fifteen people just staring at you, just you – that never happens in real life. It was a bit like magic, an extraordinary feeling, a great strain, and I found when I got down I was trembling. You are very aware of everything that's going on and you can't do anything about it.' She was still learning about the part, she says, when the play went into the studio. 'There's a moment in the statue scene when – during rehearsal I felt sure that Hermione cries when she sees her daughter. It must be a very touching thing to see your daughter alive and you haven't seen her for sixteen years. When we came to do it we did one take then we started another and I suddenly thought, "That's a very selfish thing to think – me crying! If you had a daughter you'd be more concerned not to upset her. You *are* very upset but you're not thinking about yourself, you're thinking about her!" and I did it and then I thought, "What was I doing? I wasn't crying!" Because all actors like to cry! They do! Because then they know they're feeling. So I checked with Jane and she said it was much better not crying!'

'The play is like Time's hour-glass,' says Howell. 'It comes into a waste, into blackness and darkness, then it starts to come out the other end flowering again. Because I was brought up in the country and because spring follows winter, I believe in resurrection and regrowth – not necessarily in a Christian sense, but I do believe in a cyclic thing, in the right to have second chances. And the health that comes to us through our children. Everyone has the right to a second chance and can take that right. That regenerative thing in the play kept me going. I find it the most satisfying of plays, I mean deeply, on a spiritual level, very rewarding.

'The problem with Shakespeare's plays, both on the stage and on television, is to say to your audience, "Look, my dears, I'm ever so sorry and you're probably going to hate this but you're actually going to have to listen and you're going to have to listen *all the time*. The dramatic energy is in the words – *not* in the scenery, *not* in the costumes, *not* in the cups and the daggers and the benches and the furs; it's *not there*. It's in the words, *that* is where it all takes place." The production where I first realised that – really understood it and got really excited about the words and thought, "Oh, yes, that image, they used that three scenes back!" and actually felt what it meant was Bill Gaskell's *Macbeth* at the Royal Court, which was damned by the critics but which I thought was wonderful, a major production, for its simplicity and its clarity and its focus on the actors. It was radically different from any other production I'd ever seen and I actually saw that the dramatic essence is in the words. I understood it as a piece of music. I hope people like this *Winter's Tale* and I hope they *understand* it! I'm very concerned that things should be clear, that stories should be clear: I can't bear mystification and emotional rubbish. We're telling stories to people!' She pauses, with typical self-questioning. 'People may think it's too theatrical, I don't know.' Then firmly: 'All I know is, that's what I meant it to be.'

THE BBC TV CAST AND PRODUCTION TEAM

The cast for the BBC Television production was as follows:

LEONTES	Jeremy Kemp
POLIXENES	Robert Stephens
HERMIONE	Anna Calder-Marshall
PAULINA	Margaret Tyzack
CAMILLO	David Burke
ARCHIDAMUS	John Welsh
ANTIGONUS	Cyril Luckham
AUTOLYCUS	Rikki Fulton
MAMILLIUS	Jeremy Dimmick
EMILIA	Merelina Kendall
LORD A	Leonard Kavanagh
LORD B	John Bailey
LORD C	William Relton
SERVANT TO LEONTES	Cornelius Garrett
COURT OFFICIAL	Emrys Leyshon
GAOLER/MARINER	John Benfield
CLEOMENES	John Curless
DION	Colin McCormack
SHEPHERD	Arthur Hewlett
CLOWN	Paul Jesson
FLORIZEL	Robin Kermode
PERDITA	Debbie Farrington
MOPSA	Maggie Wells
DORCAS	Janette Legge
THIRD GENTLEMAN	George Howe
CLOWN'S SERVANT	Peter Benson
SECOND LADY	Susan Broderick
PRODUCTION ASSISTANT	Val Sheppard
DIRECTOR'S ASSISTANT	Joyce Stansfeld
PRODUCTION UNIT MANAGER	Fraser Lowden

CHOREOGRAPHY	Geraldine Stephenson
MUSIC	Dudley Simpson
LITERARY CONSULTANT	John Wilders
MAKE-UP ARTIST	Cherry Alston
COSTUME DESIGNER	John Peacock
SOUND	Alan Edmonds
LIGHTING	Sam Barclay
DESIGNER	Don Homfray
SCRIPT EDITOR	David Snodin
PRODUCER	Jonathan Miller
DIRECTOR	Jane Howell

The production was recorded between 9 and 15 April 1980.

THE TEXT

The Winter's Tale, which Shakespeare based on Robert Greene's prose romance *Pandosto*, was probably written in 1611. It was first published in the 1623 Folio edition of Shakespeare's works, which included all the plays apart from *Pericles*. Subsequent folios were printed in 1632, 1663, 1664 and 1685. Nicholas Rowe, who was responsible for several stage-directions and for the division of the plays into acts and scenes, produced the first critical edition of the works in 1709. There have been numerous editions since, but the text printed here is from the late Professor Peter Alexander's famous 1951 edition of the *Complete Works*. This is the text used for all the productions in the BBC Television Shakespeare series.

Although Jonathan Miller, during his period as producer of the series, has given his directors the freedom to stray from total textual devotion on occasion, if they have felt that their interpretations need it, Jane Howell, the director of this production, has chosen to remain largely faithful to the text as printed, with only five excisions, the most notable being the exclusion of the 'Dance of the Twelve Satyrs' in Act IV Scene iv. The cuts are indicated in the right-hand margin of this printing, and also by vertical lines on either side of the text.

The marginal notes, which are designed to benefit those who might wish to compare the original text with the television production, also include the scene changes as they were presented in the camera script. These are numbered consecutively, and may on occasion differ markedly from the scenes as described in the text, either in location, or in their arrangement – sometimes a single television scene may include more than one textual scene, or vice versa. Stage-directions may differ too, and such differences are noted where they occur. There has been a slight redistribution of lines in the television production, also mentioned in the margin – most notably in the case of the Sicilian Lords, and out of fairness to the actors playing them! No mention has been made, however, of the common television practice of 'discovering' characters at the start of a scene, or of cutting away before anyone has left, even though the printed text begins each scene with the word 'enter' and ends it with 'exit' or 'exeunt', unless the characters at the opening of the scene obviously differ from those indicated in the text.

Strict followers of the words may notice the occasional but always minor divergence from complete textual fidelity on the part of individual actors in the television production. Sometimes this is a legitimate variation based on a reading of the play other than Professor Alexander's. It can, however, often be the result of the pressures of a television studio. Every effort has been made to avoid such slips, but when a scene can only be recorded three or four times at the most, the version that is chosen for transmission must always be the best in terms of performance rather than absolute textual accuracy, and even the finest actors are capable of being mildly inaccurate at the last moment!

DAVID SNODIN

THE WINTER'S TALE

DRAMATIS PERSONÆ

LEONTES, *King of Sicilia.*
MAMILLIUS, *his son, the young Prince of Sicilia.*
CAMILLO,
ANTIGONUS,
CLEOMENES, } *lords of Sicilia.*
DION,
POLIXENES, *King of Bohemia.*
FLORIZEL, *his son, Prince of Bohemia.*
ARCHIDAMUS, *a lord of Bohemia.*
OLD SHEPHERD, *reputed father of Perdita.*
CLOWN, *his son.*
AUTOLYCUS, *a rogue.*

A MARINER.
A GAOLER.
TIME, *as Chorus.*

HERMIONE, *Queen to Leontes.*
PERDITA, *daughter to Leontes and Hermione.*
PAULINA, *wife to Antigonus.*
EMILIA, *a lady attending on the Queen.*
MOPSA, } *shepherdesses.*
DORCAS,
Other LORDS, GENTLEMEN, LADIES, OFFICERS, SERVANTS, SHEPHERDS, SHEPHERDESSES.

THE SCENE : *Sicilia and Bohemia.*

ACT ONE.

SCENE I. *Sicilia. The palace of Leontes.*

Enter CAMILLO *and* ARCHIDAMUS.

SCENE I
*Exterior. Sicily.
Palace Garden. Day.*

ARCH. If you shall chance, Camillo, to visit Bohemia, on the like occasion whereon my services are now on foot, you shall see, as I have said, great difference betwixt our Bohemia and your Sicilia.

CAM. I think this coming summer the King of Sicilia means to pay Bohemia the visitation which he justly owes him.

ARCH. Wherein our entertainment shall shame us we will be justified in our loves ; for indeed—

CAM. Beseech you—   10

ARCH. Verily, I speak it in the freedom of my knowledge : we cannot with such magnificence, in so rare—I know not what to say. We will give you sleepy drinks, that your senses, unintelligent of our insufficience, may, though they cannot praise us, as little accuse us.

CAM. You pay a great deal too dear for what's given freely.

ARCH. Believe me, I speak as my understanding instructs me and as mine honesty puts it to utterance.   19

CAM. Sicilia cannot show himself overkind to Bohemia. They were train'd together in their childhoods ; and there rooted betwixt them then such an affection which cannot choose but branch now. Since their more mature dignities and royal necessities made separation of their society, their encounters, though not personal, have been royally attorneyed with interchange of gifts, letters,

loving embassies ; that they have seem'd to be together, though
absent ; shook hands, as over a vast ¦ and embrac'd as it were
from the ends of opposed winds.   The heavens continue their
loves !   30

ARCH. I think there is not in the world either malice or matter to   MAMILLIUS
alter it.   You have an unspeakable comfort of your young Prince   runs in.
Mamillius ; it is a gentleman of the greatest promise that ever
came into my note.

CAM. I very well agree with you in the hopes of him.   It is a gallant
child ; one that indeed physics the subject, makes old hearts
fresh ; they that went on crutches ere he was born desire yet their
life to see him a man.

ARCH. Would they else be content to die ?

CAM. Yes ; if there were no other excuse why they should desire to
live.   41

ARCH. If the King had no son, they would desire to live on crutches
till he had one.   [exeunt.

SCENE II.   *Sicilia.   The palace of Leontes.*

Enter LEONTES, POLIXENES, HERMIONE, MAMILLIUS, CAMILLO, *and*   In the television
ATTENDANTS.   production there is
                                                                      no change of scene.
POL. Nine changes of the wat'ry star hath been   EMILIA and a LADY
     The shepherd's note since we have left our throne   also enter.
     Without a burden.   Time as long again
     Would be fill'd up, my brother, with our thanks ;
     And yet we should for perpetuity   5
     Go hence in debt.   And therefore, like a cipher,
     Yet standing in rich place, I multiply
     With one ' We thank you ' many thousands moe
     That go before it.

LEON.   Stay your thanks a while,
     And pay them when you part.

POL.   Sir, that's to-morrow.   10
     I am question'd by my fears of what may chance
     Or breed upon our absence, that may blow
     No sneaping winds at home, to make us say
     ' This is put forth too truly '.   Besides, I have stay'd
     To tire your royalty.

LEON.   We are tougher, brother,   15
     Than you can put us to't.

POL.   No longer stay.

LEON. One sev'night longer.

POL.   Very sooth, to-morrow.

LEON. We'll part the time between's then ; and in that
     I'll no gainsaying.

POL.   Press me not, beseech you, so.
     There is no tongue that moves, none, none i' th' world,   20
     So soon as yours could win me.   So it should now,
     Were there necessity in your request, although
     'Twere needful I denied it.   My affairs
     Do even drag me homeward ; which to hinder
     Were in your love a whip to me ; my stay   25

To you a charge and trouble.   To save both,
Farewell, our brother.
LEON. Tongue-tied, our Queen ?   Speak you.
HER. I had thought, sir, to have held my peace until
You had drawn oaths from him not to stay.   You, sir,
Charge him too coldly.   Tell him you are sure   30
All in Bohemia's well—this satisfaction
The by-gone day proclaim'd.   Say this to him,
He's beat from his best ward.
LEON.   Well said, Hermione.
HER. To tell he longs to see his son were strong ;
But let him say so then, and let him go ;   35
But let him swear so, and he shall not stay ;
We'll thwack him hence with distaffs.
[to Polixenes.]   Yet of your royal presence I'll adventure
The borrow of a week.   When at Bohemia
You take my lord, I'll give him my commission   40
To let him there a month behind the gest
Prefix'd for's parting.—Yet, good deed, Leontes,
I love thee not a jar o' th' clock behind
What lady she her lord.—You'll stay ?
POL.   No, madam.
HER. Nay, but you will ?
POL.   I may not, verily.   45
HER. Verily !
You put me off with limber vows ; but I,
Though you would seek t' unsphere the stars with oaths,
Should yet say ' Sir, no going '.   Verily,
You shall not go ; a lady's ' verily ' is   50
As potent as a lord's.   Will you go yet ?
Force me to keep you as a prisoner,
Not like a guest ; so you shall pay your fees
When you depart, and save your thanks.
How say you ?
My prisoner or my guest ?   By your dread ' verily ', 55
One of them you shall be.
POL.   Your guest, then, madam :
To be your prisoner should import offending ;
Which is for me less easy to commit
Than you to punish.
HER.   Not your gaoler then,
But your kind hostess.   Come, I'll question you   60
Of my lord's tricks and yours when you were boys.
You were pretty lordings then !
POL.   We were, fair Queen,
Two lads that thought there was no more behind
But such a day to-morrow as to-day,
And to be boy eternal.
HER.   Was not my lord   65
The verier wag o' th' two ?
POL. We were as twinn'd lambs that did frisk i' th' sun
And bleat the one at th' other.   What we chang'd
Was innocence for innocence ; we knew not
The doctrine of ill-doing, nor dream'd   70

That any did.   Had we pursu'd that life,
And our weak spirits ne'er been higher rear'd
With stronger blood, we should have answer'd heaven
Boldly ' Not guilty ', the imposition clear'd
Hereditary ours.
HER.   By this we gather   75
You have tripp'd since.
POL.   O my most sacred lady,
Temptations have since then been born to 's, for
In those unfledg'd days was my wife a girl ;
Your precious self had then not cross'd the eyes
Of my young playfellow.
HER.   Grace to boot !   80
Of this make no conclusion, lest you say
Your queen and I are devils.   Yet, go on ;
Th' offences we have made you do we'll answer,
If you first sinn'd with us, and that with us
You did continue fault, and that you slipp'd not   85
With any but with us.
LEON.   Is he won yet ?
HER. He'll stay, my lord.
LEON.   At my request he would not.
Hermione, my dearest, thou never spok'st
To better purpose.
HER.   Never ?
LEON.   Never but once.
HER. What !   Have I twice said well ?   When was't before ?   90
I prithee tell me ; cram's with praise, and make's
As fat as tame things.   One good deed dying tongueless
Slaughters a thousand waiting upon that.
Our praises are our wages ; you may ride's
With one soft kiss a thousand furlongs ere   95
With spur we heat an acre.   But to th' goal :
My last good deed was to entreat his stay ;
What was my first ?   It has an elder sister,
Or I mistake you.   O, would her name were Grace !
But once before I spoke to th' purpose—When ?   100
Nay, let me have't ; I long.
LEON.   Why, that was when
Three crabbed months had sour'd themselves to death,
Ere I could make thee open thy white hand
And clap thyself my love ; then didst thou utter
' I am yours for ever '.
HER.   'Tis Grace indeed.   105
Why, lo you now, I have spoke to th' purpose twice :
The one for ever earn'd a royal husband ;
Th' other for some while a friend.
                              [*giving her hand to* POLIXENES.
LEON. [*aside.*]   Too hot, too hot !
To mingle friendship far is mingling bloods.
I have tremor cordis on me ; my heart dances,   110
But not for joy, not joy.   This entertainment
May a free face put on ; derive a liberty
From heartiness, from bounty, fertile bosom,

Jeremy Kemp as Leontes with Mamillius (Jeremy Dimmick)

And well become the agent. 'T may, I grant;
But to be paddling palms and pinching fingers,   115
As now they are, and making practis'd smiles
As in a looking-glass ; and then to sigh, as 'twere
The mort o' th' deer. O, that is entertainment
My bosom likes not, nor my brows ! Mamillius,
Art thou my boy ?
MAM.   Ay, my good lord.   120
LEON.   I' fecks !
Why, that's my bawcock. What ! hast smutch'd thy nose ?
They say it is a copy out of mine. Come, Captain,
We must be neat—not neat, but cleanly, Captain.
And yet the steer, the heifer, and the calf,
Are all call'd neat.—Still virginalling   125
Upon his palm ?—How now, you wanton calf,
Art thou my calf ?
MAM.   Yes, if you will, my lord.
LEON. Thou want'st a rough pash and the shoots that I have,
To be full like me ; yet they say we are
Almost as like as eggs. Women say so,   130
That will say any thing. But were they false
As o'er-dy'd blacks, as wind, as waters—false
As dice are to be wish'd by one that fixes
No bourn 'twixt his and mine ; yet were it true
To say this boy were like me. Come, sir page,   135
Look on me with your welkin eye. Sweet villain !
Most dear'st ! my collop ! Can thy dam ?—may't be ?
Affection ! thy intention stabs the centre.
Thou dost make possible things not so held,
Communicat'st with dreams—how can this be ?—   140
With what's unreal thou coactive art,
And fellow'st nothing. Then 'tis very credent
Thou mayst co-join with something ; and thou dost—
And that beyond commission ; and I find it,
And that to the infection of my brains   145
And hard'ning of my brows.
POL.   What means Sicilia ?
HER. He something seems unsettled.
POL.   How, my lord !
What cheer ? How is't with you, best brother ?
HER.   You look
As if you held a brow of much distraction.
Are you mov'd, my lord ?
LEON.   No, in good earnest.   150
How sometimes nature will betray its folly,
Its tenderness, and make itself a pastime
To harder bosoms ! Looking on the lines
Of my boy's face, methoughts I did recoil
Twenty-three years ; and saw myself unbreech'd,   155
In my green velvet coat ; my dagger muzzl'd,
Lest it should bite its master and so prove,
As ornaments oft do, too dangerous.
How like, methought, I then was to this kernel,
This squash, this gentleman. Mine honest friend,   160

Will you take eggs for money ?
MAM. No, my lord, I'll fight.
LEON. You will ?   Why, happy man be's dole !   My brother,
Are you so fond of your young prince as we
Do seem to be of ours ?
POL.   If at home, sir,   165
He's all my exercise, my mirth, my matter ;
Now my sworn friend, and then mine enemy ;
My parasite, my soldier, statesman, all.
He makes a July's day short as December,
And with his varying childness cures in me   170
Thoughts that would thick my blood.
LEON.   So stands this squire
Offic'd with me.   We two will walk, my lord,
And leave you to your graver steps.   Hermione,
How thou lov'st us show in our brother's welcome ;
Let what is dear in Sicily be cheap ;   175
Next to thyself and my young rover, he's
Apparent to my heart.
HER.   If you would seek us,
We are yours i' th' garden.   Shall's attend you there ?
LEON. To your own bents dispose you ; you'll be found,
Be you beneath the sky.   [aside.]   I am angling now,   180   HERMIONE and
Though you perceive me not how I give line.   POLIXENES leave at
Go to, go to !   this point.
How she holds up the neb, the bill to him !
And arms her with the boldness of a wife
To her allowing husband !
            [exeunt POLIXENES, HERMIONE, and ATTENDANTS.
                     Gone already !   185
Inch-thick, knee-deep, o'er head and ears a fork'd one !
Go, play, boy, play ; thy mother plays, and I
Play too ; but so disgrac'd a part, whose issue
Will hiss me to my grave.   Contempt and clamour
Will be my knell.   Go, play, boy, play.   There have been, 190
Or I am much deceiv'd, cuckolds ere now ;
And many a man there is, even at this present,
Now while I speak this, holds his wife by th' arm
That little thinks she has been sluic'd in's absence,
And his pond fish'd by his next neighbour, by   195
Sir Smile, his neighbour.   Nay, there's comfort in't,
Whiles other men have gates and those gates open'd,
As mine, against their will.   Should all despair
That hath revolted wives, the tenth of mankind
Would hang themselves.   Physic for't there's none ;   200
It is a bawdy planet, that will strike
Where 'tis predominant ; and 'tis pow'rful, think it,
From east, west, north, and south.   Be it concluded,
No barricado for a belly.   Know't,
It will let in and out the enemy   205
With bag and baggage.   Many thousand on's
Have the disease, and feel't not.   How now, boy !
MAM. I am like you, they say.
LEON.   Why, that's some comfort.

What! Camillo there?
CAM. Ay, my good lord.   210
LEON. Go play, Mamillius; thou'rt an honest man. [exit MAMILLIUS.
    Camillo, this great sir will yet stay longer.
CAM. You had much ado to make his anchor hold;
    When you cast out, it still came home.
LEON.   Didst note it?
CAM. He would not stay at your petitions; made   215
    His business more material.
LEON.   Didst perceive it?
    [aside.] They're here with me already; whisp'ring, rounding,
    'Sicilia is a so-forth'. 'Tis far gone
    When I shall gust it last.—How came't, Camillo,
    That he did stay?
CAM.   At the good Queen's entreaty.   220
LEON. 'At the Queen's' be't. 'Good' should be pertinent;
    But so it is, it is not. Was this taken
    By any understanding pate but thine?
    For thy conceit is soaking, will draw in
    More than the common blocks. Not noted, is't,   225
    But of the finer natures, by some severals
    Of head-piece extraordinary? Lower messes
    Perchance are to this business purblind? Say.
CAM. Business, my lord? I think most understand
    Bohemia stays here longer.
LEON.   Ha?
CAM.   Stays here longer.   230
LEON. Ay, but why?
CAM. To satisfy your Highness, and the entreaties
    Of our most gracious mistress.
LEON.   Satisfy
    Th' entreaties of your mistress! Satisfy!
    Let that suffice. I have trusted thee, Camillo,   235
    With all the nearest things to my heart, as well
    My chamber-councils, wherein, priest-like, thou
    Hast cleans'd my bosom—I from thee departed
    Thy penitent reform'd; but we have been
    Deceiv'd in thy integrity, deceiv'd   240
    In that which seems so.
CAM.   Be it forbid, my lord!
LEON. To bide upon't: thou art not honest; or,
    If thou inclin'st that way, thou art a coward,
    Which hoxes honesty behind, restraining
    From course requir'd; or else thou must be counted   245
    A servant grafted in my serious trust,
    And therein negligent; or else a fool
    That seest a game play'd home, the rich stake drawn,
    And tak'st it all for jest.
CAM.   My gracious lord,
    I may be negligent, foolish, and fearful: 250
    In every one of these no man is free
    But that his negligence, his folly, fear,
    Among the infinite doings of the world,
    Sometime puts forth. In your affairs, my lord,

If ever I were wilful-negligent,   255
It was my folly; if industriously
I play'd the fool, it was my negligence,
Not weighing well the end; if ever fearful
To do a thing where I the issue doubted,
Whereof the execution did cry out   260
Against the non-performance, 'twas a fear
Which oft infects the wisest.   These, my lord,
Are such allow'd infirmities that honesty
Is never free of.   But, beseech your Grace,
Be plainer with me; let me know my trespass   265
By its own visage; if I then deny it,
'Tis none of mine.
LEON.   Ha' not you seen, Camillo—
But that's past doubt; you have, or your eye-glass
Is thicker than a cuckold's horn—or heard—
For to a vision so apparent rumour   270
Cannot be mute—or thought—for cogitation
Resides not in that man that does not think—
My wife is slippery?   If thou wilt confess—
Or else be impudently negative,
To have nor eyes nor ears nor thought—then say   275
My wife's a hobby-horse, deserves a name
As rank as any flax-wench that puts to
Before her troth-plight.   Say't and justify't.
CAM. I would not be a stander-by to hear
My sovereign mistress clouded so, without   280
My present vengeance taken.   Shrew my heart
You never spoke what did become you less
Than this; which to reiterate were sin
As deep as that, though true.
LEON.   Is whispering nothing?
Is leaning cheek to cheek?   Is meeting noses?   285
Kissing with inside lip?   Stopping the career
Of laughter with a sigh?—a note infallible
Of breaking honesty.   Horsing foot on foot?
Skulking in corners?   Wishing clocks more swift;
Hours, minutes; noon, midnight?   And all eyes   290
Blind with the pin and web but theirs, theirs only,
That would unseen be wicked—is this nothing?
Why, then the world and all that's in't is nothing;
The covering sky is nothing; Bohemia nothing;
My wife is nothing; nor nothing have these nothings,
If this be nothing.
CAM.   Good my lord, be cur'd   296
Of this diseas'd opinion, and betimes;
For 'tis most dangerous.
LEON.   Say it be, 'tis true.
CAM. No, no, my lord.
LEON.   It is; you lie, you lie.
I say thou liest, Camillo, and I hate thee;   300
Pronounce thee a gross lout, a mindless slave,
Or else a hovering temporizer that
Canst with thine eyes at once see good and evil,

Inclining to them both.   Were my wife's liver
Infected as her life, she would not live   305
The running of one glass.
CAM.   Who does infect her ?
LEON. Why, he that wears her like her medal, hanging
    About his neck, Bohemia ; who—if I
    Had servants true about me that bare eyes
    To see alike mine honour as their profits,   310
    Their own particular thrifts, they would do that
    Which should undo more doing.   Ay, and thou,
    His cupbearer—whom I from meaner form
    Have bench'd and rear'd to worship ; who mayst see,
    Plainly as heaven sees earth and earth sees heaven,   315
    How I am gall'd—mightst bespice a cup
    To give mine enemy a lasting wink ;
    Which draught to me were cordial.
CAM.   Sir, my lord,
    I could do this ; and that with no rash potion,
    But with a ling'ring dram that should not work   320
    Maliciously like poison.   But I cannot
    Believe this crack to be in my dread mistress,
    So sovereignly being honourable.
    I have lov'd thee—
LEON. Make that thy question, and go rot !
    Dost think I am so muddy, so unsettled,   325
    To appoint myself in this vexation ; sully
    The purity and whiteness of my sheets—
    Which to preserve is sleep, which being spotted
    Is goads, thorns, nettles, tails of wasps ;
    Give scandal to the blood o' th' Prince, my son—   330
    Who I do think is mine, and love as mine—
    Without ripe moving to 't ?   Would I do this ?
    Could man so blench ?
CAM.   I must believe you, sir.
    I do ; and will fetch off Bohemia for't ;
    Provided that, when he's remov'd, your Highness   335
    Will take again your queen as yours at first,
    Even for your son's sake ; and thereby for sealing
    The injury of tongues in courts and kingdoms
    Known and allied to yours.
LEON.   Thou dost advise me
    Even so as I mine own course have set down.   340
    I'll give no blemish to her honour, none.
CAM. My lord,
    Go then ; and with a countenance as clear
    As friendship wears at feasts, keep with Bohemia
    And with your queen.   I am his cupbearer ;   345
    If from me he have wholesome beverage,
    Account me not your servant.
LEON.   This is all :
    Do't, and thou hast the one half of my heart ;
    Do't not, thou split'st thine own.
CAM.   I'll do't, my lord.   349
LEON. I will seem friendly, as thou hast advis'd me.   [exit.

Lines 319–321, 'and
that . . . like poison',
omitted.

CAM. O miserable lady! But, for me,
What case stand I in? I must be the poisoner
Of good Polixenes; and my ground to do't
Is the obedience to a master; one
Who, in rebellion with himself, will have   355
All that are his so too. To do this deed,
Promotion follows. If I could find example
Of thousands that had struck anointed kings
And flourish'd after, I'd not do't; but since
Nor brass, nor stone, nor parchment, bears not one,   360
Let villainy itself forswear't. I must
Forsake the court. To do't, or no, is certain
To me a break-neck. Happy star reign now!
Here comes Bohemia.

Enter POLIXENES.

POL.   This is strange. Methinks
My favour here begins to warp. Not speak?   365
Good day, Camillo.
CAM.   Hail, most royal sir!
POL. What is the news i' th' court?
CAM.   None rare, my lord.
POL. The King hath on him such a countenance
As he had lost some province, and a region
Lov'd as he loves himself; even now I met him   370
With customary compliment, when he,
Wafting his eyes to th' contrary and falling
A lip of much contempt, speeds from me;
So leaves me to consider what is breeding
That changes thus his manners.   375
CAM. I dare not know, my lord.
POL. How, dare not! Do not. Do you know, and dare not
Be intelligent to me? 'Tis thereabouts;
For, to yourself, what you do know, you must,
And cannot say you dare not. Good Camillo,   380
Your chang'd complexions are to me a mirror
Which shows me mine chang'd too; for I must be
A party in this alteration, finding
Myself thus alter'd with't.
CAM.   There is a sickness
Which puts some of us in distemper; but   385
I cannot name the disease; and it is caught
Of you that yet are well.
POL.   How! caught of me?
Make me not sighted like the basilisk;
I have look'd on thousands who have sped the better
By my regard, but kill'd none so. Camillo—   390
As you are certainly a gentleman; thereto
Clerk-like experienc'd, which no less adorns
Our gentry than our parents' noble names,
In whose success we are gentle—I beseech you,
If you know aught which does behove my knowledge   395
Thereof to be inform'd, imprison't not
In ignorant concealment.

CAM.　　　　　　　　　　I may not answer.
POL. A sickness caught of me, and yet I well?
　I must be answer'd.　Dost thou hear, Camillo?
　I conjure thee, by all the parts of man　　　　　　　　400
　Which honour does acknowledge, whereof the least
　Is not this suit of mine, that thou declare
　What incidency thou dost guess of harm
　Is creeping toward me; how far off, how near;
　Which way to be prevented, if to be;　　　　　　　　405
　If not, how best to bear it.
CAM.　　　　　　　　　Sir, I will tell you;
　Since I am charg'd in honour, and by him
　That I think honourable.　Therefore mark my counsel,
　Which must be ev'n as swiftly followed as
　I mean to utter it, or both yourself and me　　　　　410
　Cry lost, and so goodnight.
POL.　　　　　　　　On, good Camillo.
CAM. I am appointed him to murder you.
POL. By whom, Camillo?
CAM.　　　　　　　　By the King.
POL.　　　　　　　　　For what?
CAM. He thinks, nay, with all confidence he swears,
　As he had seen 't or been an instrument　　　　　　415
　To vice you to't, that you have touch'd his queen
　Forbiddenly.
POL.　　　　　　　O, then my best blood turn
　To an infected jelly, and my name
　Be yok'd with his that did betray the Best!
　Turn then my freshest reputation to　　　　　　　420
　A savour that may strike the dullest nostril
　Where I arrive, and my approach be shunn'd,
　Nay, hated too, worse than the great'st infection
　That e'er was heard or read!
CAM.　　　　　　　　Swear his thought over
　By each particular star in heaven and　　　　　　　425
　By all their influences, you may as well
　Forbid the sea for to obey the moon
　As or by oath remove or counsel shake
　The fabric of his folly, whose foundation
　Is pil'd upon his faith and will continue　　　　　430
　The standing of his body.
POL.　　　　　　　　How should this grow?
CAM. I know not; but I am sure 'tis safer to
　Avoid what's grown than question how 'tis born.
　If therefore you dare trust my honesty,
　That lies enclosed in this trunk which you　　　　　435
　Shall bear along impawn'd, away to-night.
　Your followers I will whisper to the business;
　And will, by twos and threes, at several posterns,
　Clear them o' th' city.　For myself, I'll put
　My fortunes to your service, which are here　　　　440
　By this discovery lost.　Be not uncertain,
　For, by the honour of my parents, I
　Have utt'red truth; which if you seek to prove,

I dare not stand by ; nor shall you be safer
Than one condemn'd by the King's own mouth, thereon
His execution sworn.

POL.   I do believe thee :   446
I saw his heart in's face. Give me thy hand ;
Be pilot to me, and thy places shall
Still neighbour mine. My ships are ready, and
My people did expect my hence departure   450
Two days ago. This jealousy
Is for a precious creature ; as she's rare,
Must it be great ; and, as his person's mighty,
Must it be violent ; and as he does conceive
He is dishonour'd by a man which ever   455
Profess'd to him, why, his revenges must
In that be made more bitter. Fear o'ershades me.
Good expedition be my friend, and comfort
The gracious Queen, part of this theme, but nothing
Of his ill-ta'en suspicion ! Come, Camillo ;   460
I will respect thee as a father, if
Thou bear'st my life off hence. Let us avoid.

CAM. It is in mine authority to command
The keys of all the posterns. Please your Highness
To take the urgent hour. Come, sir, away.   [*exeunt.*

ACT TWO.

SCENE I.   *Sicilia.*   *The palace of Leontes.*

Enter HERMIONE, MAMILLIUS, *and* LADIES.

SCENE 2
Exterior. Sicily.
Palace Garden. Day.
I LADY is played by
EMILIA.

HER. Take the boy to you ; he so troubles me,
'Tis past enduring.

I LADY.   Come, my gracious lord,   EMILIA.
Shall I be your playfellow ?

MAM.   No, I'll none of you.

I LADY. Why, my sweet lord ?   EMILIA.

MAM. You'll kiss me hard, and speak to me as if   5
I were a baby still. I love you better.

2 LADY. And why so, my lord ?

MAM.   Not for because
Your brows are blacker ; yet black brows, they say,
Become some women best ; so that there be not
Too much hair there, but in a semicircle   10
Or a half-moon made with a pen.

2 LADY.   Who taught't this ?

MAM. I learn'd it out of women's faces. Pray now,
What colour are your eyebrows ?

I LADY.   Blue, my lord.   EMILIA.

MAM. Nay, that's a mock. I have seen a lady's nose
That has been blue, but not her eyebrows.

I LADY.   Hark ye :   15   EMILIA.
The Queen your mother rounds apace. We shall
Present our services to a fine new prince
One of these days ; and then you'd wanton with us,
If we would have you.

2 LADY.   She is spread of late
    Into a goodly bulk. Good time encounter her !   20
HER. What wisdom stirs amongst you ? Come, sir, now
    I am for you again. Pray you sit by us,
    And tell's a tale.
MAM.   Merry or sad shall't be ?
HER. As merry as you will.
MAM. A sad tale's best for winter. I have one   25
    Of sprites and goblins.
HER.   Let's have that, good sir.
    Come on, sit down ; come on, and do your best
    To fright me with your sprites ; you're pow'rful at it.
MAM. There was a man—
HER.   Nay, come, sit down ; then on.
MAM. Dwelt by a churchyard—I will tell it softly ;   30
    Yond crickets shall not hear it.
HER.   Come on then,
    And give't me in mine ear.

        Enter LEONTES, ANTIGONUS, LORDS *and* OTHERS.

LEON. Was he met there ? his train ? Camillo with him ?
1 LORD. Behind the tuft of pines I met them ; never
    Saw I men scour so on their way. I ey'd them   35
    Even to their ships.
LEON.   How blest am I
    In my just censure, in my true opinion !
    Alack, for lesser knowledge ! How accurs'd
    In being so blest ! There may be in the cup
    A spider steep'd, and one may drink, depart,   40
    And yet partake no venom, for his knowledge
    Is not infected ; but if one present
    Th' abhorr'd ingredient to his eye, make known
    How he hath drunk, he cracks his gorge, his sides,
    With violent hefts. I have drunk, and seen the spider.   45
    Camillo was his help in this, his pander.
    There is a plot against my life, my crown ;
    All's true that is mistrusted. That false villain
    Whom I employ'd was pre-employ'd by him ;
    He has discover'd my design, and I   50
    Remain a pinch'd thing ; yea, a very trick
    For them to play at will. How came the posterns
    So easily open ?
1 LORD. By his great authority ;
    Which often hath no less prevail'd than so
    On your command.
LEON.   I know't too well.   55
    Give me the boy. I am glad you did not nurse him ;
    Though he does bear some signs of me, yet you
    Have too much blood in him.
HER.   What is this ? Sport ?
LEON. Bear the boy hence ; he shall not come about her ;
    Away with him ; and let her sport herself   60
                [MAMILLIUS *is led out.*

    With that she's big with—for 'tis Polixenes
    Has made thee swell thus.
HER.   But I'd say he had not,
    And I'll be sworn you would believe my saying,
    Howe'er you lean to th' nayward.
LEON.   You, my lords,
    Look on her, mark her well ; be but about   65
    To say ' She is a goodly lady ' and
    The justice of your hearts will thereto add
    ' 'Tis pity she's not honest—honourable '.
    Praise her but for this her without-door form,
    Which on my faith deserves high speech, and straight   70
    The shrug, the hum or ha, these petty brands
    That calumny doth use—O, I am out !—
    That mercy does, for calumny will sear
    Virtue itself—these shrugs, these hum's and ha's,
    When you have said she's goodly, come between,   75
    Ere you can say she's honest. But be't known,
    From him that has most cause to grieve it should be,
    She's an adultress.
HER.   Should a villain say so,
    The most replenish'd villain in the world,
    He were as much more villain : you, my lord,   80
    Do but mistake.
LEON.   You have mistook, my lady,
    Polixenes for Leontes. O thou thing !
    Which I'll not call a creature of thy place,
    Lest barbarism, making me the precedent,
    Should a like language use to all degrees   85
    And mannerly distinguishment leave out
    Betwixt the prince and beggar. I have said
    She's an adultress ; I have said with whom.
    More, she's a traitor ; and Camillo is
    A federary with her, and one that knows   90
    What she should shame to know herself
    But with her most vile principal—that she's
    A bed-swerver, even as bad as those
    That vulgars give bold'st titles ; ay, and privy
    To this their late escape.
HER.   No, by my life,   95
    Privy to none of this. How will this grieve you,
    When you shall come to clearer knowledge, that
    You thus have publish'd me ! Gentle my lord,
    You scarce can right me throughly then to say
    You did mistake.
LEON.   No ; if I mistake   100
    In those foundations which I build upon,
    The centre is not big enough to bear
    A school-boy's top. Away with her to prison.
    He who shall speak for her is afar off guilty
    But that he speaks.
HER.   There's some ill planet reigns.   105
    I must be patient till the heavens look
    With an aspect more favourable. Good my lords,

I am not prone to weeping, as our sex
Commonly are—the want of which vain dew
Perchance shall dry your pities—but I have   110
That honourable grief lodg'd here which burns
Worse than tears drown. Beseech you all, my lords,
With thoughts so qualified as your charities
Shall best instruct you, measure me ;   and so
The King's will be perform'd !
LEON. [to the Guard.]   Shall I be heard ?   115
HER. Who is't that goes with me ?   Beseech your highness
My women may be with me, for you see
My plight requires it.   Do not weep, good fools ;
There is no cause ; when you shall know your mistress
Has deserv'd prison, then abound in tears   120
As I come out : this action I now go on
Is for my better grace.   Adieu, my lord.
I never wish'd to see you sorry ;   now
I trust I shall.   My women, come ;   you have leave.
LEON. Go, do our bidding ; hence !   125
                    [exeunt HERMIONE, guarded, and LADIES.
I LORD. Beseech your Highness, call the Queen again.   2 LORD.
ANT. Be certain what you do, sir, lest your justice
Prove violence, in the which three great ones suffer,
Yourself, your queen, your son.
I LORD.   For her, my lord,   3 LORD.
I dare my life lay down—and will do't, sir,
Please you t' accept it—that the Queen is spotless   130
I' th' eyes of heaven and to you—I mean
In this which you accuse her.
ANT.   If it prove
She's otherwise, I'll keep my stables where
I lodge my wife ;   I'll go in couples with her ;
Than when I feel and see her no farther trust her ;   135
For every inch of woman in the world,
Ay, every dram of woman's flesh is false,
If she be.
LEON. Hold your peaces.
I LORD.   Good my lord—   2 LORD.
ANT. It is for you we speak, not for ourselves.   140
You are abus'd, and by some putter-on
That will be damn'd for't.   Would I knew the villain !
I would land-damn him.   Be she honour-flaw'd—
I have three daughters :   the eldest is eleven ;
The second and the third, nine and some five ;   145
If this prove true, they'll pay for't.   By mine honour,
I'll geld 'em all ;   fourteen they shall not see
To bring false generations.   They are co-heirs ;
And I had rather glib myself than they
Should not produce fair issue.
LEON.   Cease ;   no more   150
You smell this business with a sense as cold
As is a dead man's nose ; but I do see't and feel't
As you feel doing thus ;   and see withal
The instruments that feel.

ANT.   If it be so,
  We need no grave to bury honesty;   155
  There's not a grain of it the face to sweeten
  Of the whole dungy earth.
LEON.   What! Lack I credit?
1 LORD. I had rather you did lack than I, my lord,   2 LORD.
  Upon this ground; and more it would content me
  To have her honour true than your suspicion,   160
  Be blam'd for't how you might.
LEON.   Why, what need we
  Commune with you of this, but rather follow
  Our forceful instigation? Our prerogative
  Calls not your counsels; but our natural goodness
  Imparts this; which, if you—or stupified   165
  Or seeming so in skill—cannot or will not
  Relish a truth like us, inform yourselves
  We need no more of your advice. The matter,
  The loss, the gain, the ord'ring on't, is all
  Properly ours.
ANT.   And I wish, my liege,   170
  You had only in your silent judgment tried it,
  Without more overture.
LEON.   How could that be?
  Either thou art most ignorant by age,
  Or thou wert born a fool. Camillo's flight,
  Added to their familiarity—   175
  Which was as gross as ever touch'd conjecture,
  That lack'd sight only, nought for approbation
  But only seeing, all other circumstances
  Made up to th' deed—doth push on this proceeding.
  Yet, for a greater confirmation—   180
  For, in an act of this importance, 'twere
  Most piteous to be wild—I have dispatch'd in post
  To sacred Delphos, to Apollo's temple,
  Cleomenes and Dion, whom you know
  Of stuff'd sufficiency. Now, from the oracle   185
  They will bring all, whose spiritual counsel had
  Shall stop or spur me. Have I done well?
1 LORD. Well done, my lord.   3 LORD.
LEON. Though I am satisfied, and need no more
  Than what I know, yet shall the oracle   190
  Give rest to th' minds of others such as he
  Whose ignorant credulity will not
  Come up to th' truth. So have we thought it good
  From our free person she should be confin'd,
  Lest that the treachery of the two fled hence   195
  Be left her to perform. Come, follow us;
  We are to speak in public; for this business
  Will raise us all.
ANT. [aside.] To laughter, as I take it,
  If the good truth were known.   [exeunt.

SCENE II. *Sicilia. A prison.*

Enter PAULINA, *a* GENTLEMAN, *and* ATTENDANTS.

SCENE 3
*Interior. Sicily.
A Prison. Night.*
GENTLEMAN is played
by PAULINA'S
STEWARD.

PAUL. The keeper of the prison—call to him ;
    Let him have knowledge who I am.   [*exit* GENTLEMAN.
                       Good lady !
    No court in Europe is too good for thee ;
    What dost thou then in prison ?

Re-enter GENTLEMAN *with the* GAOLER.

                     Now, good sir,
    You know me, do you not ?
GAOL.   For a worthy lady,   5
    And one who much I honour.
PAUL.   Pray you, then,
    Conduct me to the Queen.
GAOL.   I may not, madam ;
    To the contrary I have express commandment.
PAUL. Here's ado, to lock up honesty and honour from
    Th' access of gentle visitors ! Is't lawful, pray you,
    To see her women—any of them ? Emilia ?
GAOL. So please you, madam,
    To put apart these your attendants, I
    Shall bring Emilia forth.
PAUL.   I pray now, call her.   15
    Withdraw yourselves.   [*exeunt* ATTENDANTS.
GAOL.   And, madam,
    I must be present at your conference.
PAUL. Well, be't so, prithee.   [*exit* GAOLER.
    Here's such ado to make no stain a stain
    As passes colouring.

Re-enter GAOLER, *with* EMILIA.

               Dear gentlewoman,   20
    How fares our gracious lady ?
EMIL. As well as one so great and so forlorn
    May hold together. On her frights and griefs,
    Which never tender lady hath borne greater,
    She is, something before her time, deliver'd.   25
PAUL. A boy ?
EMIL. A daughter, and a goodly babe,
    Lusty, and like to live. The Queen receives
    Much comfort in't ; says ' My poor prisoner,
    I am as innocent as you '.
PAUL.   I dare be sworn.
    These dangerous unsafe lunes i' th' King, beshrew them ! 30
    He must be told on't, and he shall. The office
    Becomes a woman best ; I'll take't upon me ;
    If I prove honey-mouth'd, let my tongue blister,
    And never to my red-look'd anger be
    The trumpet any more. Pray you, Emilia,   35
    Commend my best obedience to the Queen ;
    If she dares trust me with her little babe,
    I'll show't the King, and undertake to be

Merelina Kendall as Emilia and Margaret Tyzack as Paulina

Her advocate to th' loud'st.   We do not know
How he may soften at the sight o' th' child :   40
The silence often of pure innocence
Persuades when speaking fails.
EMIL.   Most worthy madam,
Your honour and your goodness is so evident
That your free undertaking cannot miss
A thriving issue ; there is no lady living   45
So meet for this great errand.   Please your ladyship
To visit the next room, I'll presently
Acquaint the Queen of your most noble offer
Who but to-day hammer'd of this design,
But durst not tempt a minister of honour,   50
Lest she should be denied.
PAUL.   Tell her, Emilia,
I'll use that tongue I have ; if wit flow from't
As boldness from my bosom, let't not be doubted
I shall do good.
EMIL.   Now be you blest for it !
I'll to the Queen.   Please you come something nearer.   55
GAOL. Madam, if't please the Queen to send the babe,
I know not what I shall incur to pass it,
Having no warrant.
PAUL.   You need not fear it, sir.
This child was prisoner to the womb, and is
By law and process of great Nature thence   60
Freed and enfranchis'd—not a party to
The anger of the King, nor guilty of,
If any be, the trespass of the Queen.
GAOL. I do believe it.
PAUL. Do not you fear.   Upon mine honour, I   65
Will stand betwixt you and danger.   [exeunt.

SCENE III.   Sicilia.   The palace of Leontes.

Enter LEONTES, ANTIGONUS, LORDS, and SERVANTS.

LEON. Nor night nor day no rest !   It is but weakness
To bear the matter thus—mere weakness.   If
The cause were not in being—part o' th' cause,
She, th' adultress ; for the harlot king
Is quite beyond mine arm, out of the blank   5
And level of my brain, plot-proof ; but she
I can hook to me—say that she were gone,
Given to the fire, a moiety of my rest
Might come to me again.   Who's there ?
I SERV.   My lord ?
LEON. How does the boy ?
I SERV.   He took good rest to-night ; 10
'Tis hop'd his sickness is discharg'd.
LEON. To see his nobleness !
Conceiving the dishonour of his mother,
He straight declin'd, droop'd, took it deeply,
Fasten'd and fix'd the shame on't in himself,   15
Threw off his spirit, his appetite, his sleep,

SCENE 4
Interior. Sicily.
Palace. Night.
LEONTES alone.

SERVANT enters here.

51

And downright languish'd. Leave me solely. Go,
See how he fares. [*exit* SERVANT.] Fie, fie! no thought of him!
The very thought of my revenges that way
Recoil upon me—in himself too mighty,   20
And in his parties, his alliance. Let him be,
Until a time may serve; for present vengeance,
Take it on her. Camillo and Polixenes
Laugh at me, make their pastime at my sorrow.
They should not laugh if I could reach them; nor   25
Shall she, within my pow'r.

                  Enter PAULINA, *with a* CHILD.   PAULINA enters,
                                                                      restrained by
1 LORD.   You must not enter.   ANTIGONUS and other
PAUL. Nay, rather, good my lords, be second to me.   Lords.
    Fear you his tyrannous passion more, alas,
    Than the Queen's life? A gracious innocent soul,
    More free than he is jealous.
ANT.   That's enough.   30
2 SERV. Madam, he hath not slept to-night; commanded
    None should come at him.
PAUL.   Not so hot, good sir;
    I come to bring him sleep. 'Tis such as you,
    That creep like shadows by him, and do sigh
    At each his needless heavings—such as you   35
    Nourish the cause of his awaking: I
    Do come with words as medicinal as true,
    Honest as either, to purge him of that humour
    That presses him from sleep.
LEON.   What noise there, ho?
PAUL. No noise, my lord; but needful conference   40
    About some gossips for your Highness.
LEON.   How!
    Away with that audacious lady! Antigonus,
    I charg'd thee that she should not come about me;
    I knew she would.
ANT.   I told her so, my lord,
    On your displeasure's peril, and on mine,   45
    She should not visit you.
LEON.   What, canst not rule her?
PAUL. From all dishonesty he can: in this,
    Unless he take the course that you have done—
    Commit me for committing honour—trust it,
    He shall not rule me.
ANT.   La you now, you hear!   50
    When she will take the rein, I let her run;
    But she'll not stumble.
PAUL.   Good my liege, I come—
    And I beseech you hear me, who professes
    Myself your loyal servant, your physician,
    Your most obedient counsellor; yet that dares   55
    Less appear so, in comforting your evils,
    Than such as most seem yours—I say I come
    From your good Queen.
LEON. Good Queen!

PAUL. Good Queen, my lord, good Queen—I say good Queen ;
    And would by combat make her good, so were I   60
    A man, the worst about you.
LEON.   Force her hence.
PAUL. Let him that makes but trifles of his eyes
    First hand me.   On mine own accord I'll off ;
    But first I'll do my errand.   The good Queen,
    For she is good, hath brought you forth a daughter ;   65
    Here 'tis ;   commends it to your blessing.   [laying down the child.
LEON.   Out !
    A mankind witch !   Hence with her, out o' door !
    A most intelligencing bawd !
PAUL.   Not so.
    I am as ignorant in that as you
    In so entitling me ;   and no less honest   70
    Than you are mad ;   which is enough, I'll warrant,
    As this world goes, to pass for honest.
LEON.   Traitors !
    Will you not push her out ?   Give her the bastard.
    [to Antigonus.]   Thou dotard, thou art woman-tir'd, unroosted
    By thy Dame Partlet here.   Take up the bastard ;   75
    Take't up, I say ;   give't to thy crone.
PAUL.   For ever
    Unvenerable be thy hands, if thou
    Tak'st up the Princess by that forced baseness
    Which he has put upon't !
LEON.   He dreads his wife.
PAUL. So I would you did ;   then 'twere past all doubt   80
    You'd call your children yours.
LEON.   A nest of traitors !
ANT. I am none, by this good light.
PAUL.   Nor I ;   nor any
    But one that's here ;   and that's himself ;   for he
    The sacred honour of himself, his Queen's,
    His hopeful son's, his babe's, betrays to slander,   85
    Whose sting is sharper than the sword's ;   and will not—
    For, as the case now stands, it is a curse
    He cannot be compell'd to 't—once remove
    The root of his opinion, which is rotten
    As ever oak or stone was sound.
LEON.   A callat   90
    Of boundless tongue, who late hath beat her husband,
    And now baits me !   This brat is none of mine ;
    It is the issue of Polixenes.
    Hence with it, and together with the dam
    Commit them to the fire.
PAUL.   It is yours.   95
    And, might we lay th' old proverb to your charge,
    So like you 'tis the worse.   Behold, my lords,
    Although the print be little, the whole matter
    And copy of the father—eye, nose, lip,
    The trick of 's frown, his forehead ;   nay, the valley,   100
    The pretty dimples of his chin and cheek ;   his smiles ;
    The very mould and frame of hand, nail, finger.

And thou, good goddess Nature, which hast made it
So like to him that got it, if thou hast
The ordering of the mind too, 'mongst all colours   105
No yellow in't, lest she suspect, as he does,
Her children not her husband's!
LEON.   A gross hag!
And, lozel, thou art worthy to be hang'd
That wilt not stay her tongue.
ANT.   Hang all the husbands
That cannot do that feat, you'll leave yourself   110
Hardly one subject.
LEON.   Once more, take her hence.
PAUL. A most unworthy and unnatural lord
Can do no more.
LEON.   I'll ha' thee burnt.
PAUL.   I care not.
It is an heretic that makes the fire,
Not she which burns in't.   I'll not call you tyrant: 115
But this most cruel usage of your Queen—
Not able to produce more accusation
Than your own weak-hing'd fancy—something savours
Of tyranny, and will ignoble make you,
Yea, scandalous to the world.
LEON.   On your allegiance,   120
Out of the chamber with her!   Were I a tyrant,
Where were her life?   She durst not call me so,
If she did know me one.   Away with her!
PAUL. I pray you, do not push me; I'll be gone.
Look to your babe, my lord; 'tis yours.   Jove send her   125
A better guiding spirit!   What needs these hands?
You that are thus so tender o'er his follies
Will never do him good, not one of you.
So, so.   Farewell; we are gone.   [exit.
LEON. Thou, traitor, hast set on thy wife to this.   130
My child!   Away with't.   Even thou, that hast
A heart so tender o'er it, take it hence,
And see it instantly consum'd with fire;
Even thou, and none but thou.   Take it up straight.
Within this hour bring me word 'tis done,   135
And by good testimony, or I'll seize thy life,
With that thou else call'st thine.   If thou refuse,
And wilt encounter with my wrath, say so;
The bastard brains with these my proper hands
Shall I dash out.   Go, take it to the fire;   140
For thou set'st on thy wife.
ANT.   I did not, sir.
These lords, my noble fellows, if they please,
Can clear me in't.
LORDS.   We can.   My royal liege,   1 LORD.
He is not guilty of her coming hither.
LEON. You're liars all.   145
1 LORD. Beseech your Highness, give us better credit.   2 LORD.
We have always truly serv'd you; and beseech
So to esteem of us; and on our knees we beg,

As recompense of our dear services
Past and to come, that you do change this purpose,   150
Which being so horrible, so bloody, must
Lead on to some foul issue. We all kneel.
LEON. I am a feather for each wind that blows.
  Shall I live on to see this bastard kneel
  And call me father? Better burn it now   155
  Than curse it then. But be it; let it live.
  It shall not neither. [*to* ANTIGONUS.]   You, sir, come you hither.
  You that have been so tenderly officious
  With Lady Margery, your midwife there,
  To save this bastard's life—for 'tis a bastard,   160
  So sure as this beard's grey—what will you adventure
  To save this brat's life?
ANT.   Anything, my lord,
  That my ability may undergo,
  And nobleness impose. At least, thus much:
  I'll pawn the little blood which I have left   165
  To save the innocent—anything possible.
LEON. It shall be possible. Swear by this sword
  Thou wilt perform my bidding.
ANT.   I will, my lord.
LEON. Mark, and perform it—seest thou? For the fail
  Of any point in't shall not only be   170
  Death to thyself, but to thy lewd-tongu'd wife,
  Whom for this time we pardon.   We enjoin thee,
  As thou art liegeman to us, that thou carry
  This female bastard hence; and that thou bear it
  To some remote and desert place, quite out   175
  Of our dominions; and that there thou leave it,
  Without more mercy, to it own protection
  And favour of the climate. As by strange fortune
  It came to us, I do in justice charge thee,
  On thy soul's peril and thy body's torture,   180
  That thou commend it strangely to some place
  Where chance may nurse or end it. Take it up.
ANT. I swear to do this, though a present death
  Had been more merciful. Come on, poor babe.
  Some powerful spirit instruct the kites and ravens   185
  To be thy nurses! Wolves and bears, they say,
  Casting their savageness aside, have done
  Like offices of pity. Sir, be prosperous
  In more than this deed does require! And blessing
  Against this cruelty fight on thy side,   190
  Poor thing, condemn'd to loss!   [*exit with the child.*
LEON.   No, I'll not rear
  Another's issue.

Enter a SERVANT.

SERV.   Please your Highness, posts
  From those you sent to th' oracle are come
  An hour since. Cleomenes and Dion,
  Being well arriv'd from Delphos, are both landed,   195
  Hasting to th' court.

1 LORD. So please you, sir, their speed
   Hath been beyond account.
LEON.   Twenty-three days
   They have been absent ; 'tis good speed ; foretells
   The great Apollo suddenly will have
   The truth of this appear. Prepare you, lords ;   200
   Summon a session, that we may arraign
   Our most disloyal lady ; for, as she hath
   Been publicly accus'd, so shall she have
   A just and open trial. While she lives,
   My heart will be a burden to me. Leave me ;   205
   And think upon my bidding.   [*exeunt.*

ACT THREE.

SCENE I. *Sicilia. On the road to the Capital.*

Enter CLEOMENES *and* DION.

SCENE 5
*Exterior. Sicily.
A Road. Day.*
The Indictment
against Hermione is
nailed to a tree.

CLEO. The climate's delicate, the air most sweet,
   Fertile the isle, the temple much surpassing
   The common praise it bears.
DION.   I shall report,
   For most it caught me, the celestial habits—
   Methinks I so should term them—and the reverence   5
   Of the grave wearers. O, the sacrifice !
   How ceremonious, solemn, and unearthly,
   It was i' th' off'ring !
CLEO.   But of all, the burst
   And the ear-deaf'ning voice o' th' oracle,
   Kin to Jove's thunder, so surpris'd my sense   10
   That I was nothing.
DION.   If th' event o' th' journey
   Prove as successful to the Queen—O, be't so !—
   As it hath been to us rare, pleasant, speedy,
   The time is worth the use on't.
CLEO.   Great Apollo
   Turn all to th' best ! These proclamations,   15
   So forcing faults upon Hermione,
   I little like.
DION.   The violent carriage of it
   Will clear or end the business. When the oracle—
   Thus by Apollo's great divine seal'd up—
   Shall the contents discover, something rare   20
   Even then will rush to knowledge. Go ; fresh horses.
   And gracious be the issue !   [*exeunt.*

SCENE II. *Sicilia. A court of justice.*

Enter LEONTES, LORDS, *and* OFFICERS.

SCENE 6
*Exterior. Sicily.
Palace Garden (set for
Trial). Day.*
In the television
production all the
major characters,
including HERMIONE
and PAULINA, are
present from the start
of the scene.

LEON. This sessions, to our great grief we pronounce,
   Even pushes 'gainst our heart—the party tried,
   The daughter of a king, our wife, and one
   Of us too much belov'd. Let us be clear'd
   Of being tyrannous, since we so openly   5
   Proceed in justice, which shall have due course,

Even to the guilt or the purgation.
Produce the prisoner.
OFFI. It is his Highness' pleasure that the Queen
Appear in person here in court.

Enter HERMIONE, *as to her trial,* PAULINA, *and* LADIES.   They move forward.
Silence !   10
LEON. Read the indictment.
OFFI. [*reads.*] ' Hermione, Queen to the worthy Leontes, King of
Sicilia, thou art here accused and arraigned of high treason, in
committing adultery with Polixenes, King of Bohemia ; and
conspiring with Camillo to take away the life of our sovereign
lord the King, thy royal husband : the pretence whereof being by
circumstances partly laid open, thou, Hermione, contrary to the
faith and allegiance of a true subject, didst counsel and aid them,
for their better safety, to fly away by night.'
HER. Since what I am to say must be but that   20
Which contradicts my accusation, and
The testimony on my part no other
But what comes from myself, it shall scarce boot me
To say ' Not guilty '.   Mine integrity
Being counted falsehood shall, as I express it,   25
Be so receiv'd.   But thus—if pow'rs divine
Behold our human actions, as they do,
I doubt not then but innocence shall make
False accusation blush, and tyranny
Tremble at patience.   You, my lord, best know—   30
Who least will seem to do so—my past life
Hath been as continent, as chaste, as true,
As I am now unhappy ; which is more
Than history can pattern, though devis'd
And play'd to take spectators ; for behold me—   35
A fellow of the royal bed, which owe
A moiety of the throne, a great king's daughter,
The mother to a hopeful prince—here standing
To prate and talk for life and honour fore
Who please to come and hear.   For life, I prize it   40
As I weigh grief, which I would spare ; for honour,
'Tis a derivative from me to mine,
And only that I stand for.   I appeal
To your own conscience, sir, before Polixenes
Came to your court, how I was in your grace,   45
How merited to be so ; since he came,
With what encounter so uncurrent I
Have strain'd t' appear thus ; if one jot beyond
The bound of honour, or in act or will
That way inclining, hard'ned be the hearts   50
Of all that hear me, and my near'st of kin
Cry fie upon my grave !
LEON.   I ne'er heard yet
That any of these bolder vices wanted
Less impudence to gainsay what they did
Than to perform it first.
HER.   That's true enough ;   55
Though 'tis a saying, sir, not due to me.

LEON. You will not own it.
HER.   More than mistress of
    Which comes to me in name of fault, I must not
    At all acknowledge. For Polixenes,
    With whom I am accus'd, I do confess   60
    I lov'd him as in honour he requir'd ;
    With such a kind of love as might become
    A lady like me ; with a love even such,
    So and no other, as yourself commanded ;
    Which not to have done, I think had been in me   65
    Both disobedience and ingratitude
    To you and toward your friend ; whose love had spoke,
    Even since it could speak, from an infant, freely,
    That it was yours. Now for conspiracy :
    I know not how it tastes, though it be dish'd   70
    For me to try how ; all I know of it
    Is that Camillo was an honest man ;
    And why he left your court, the gods themselves,
    Wotting no more than I, are ignorant.
LEON. You knew of his departure, as you know   75
    What you have underta'en to do in's absence.
HER. Sir,
    You speak a language that I understand not.
    My life stands in the level of your dreams,
    Which I'll lay down.
LEON.   Your actions are my dreams.   80
    You had a bastard by Polixenes,
    And I but dream'd it. As you were past all shame—
    Those of your fact are so—so past all truth ;
    Which to deny concerns more than avails ; for as
    Thy brat hath been cast out, like to itself,   85
    No father owning it—which is indeed
    More criminal in thee than it—so thou
    Shalt feel our justice ; in whose easiest passage
    Look for no less than death.
HER.   Sir, spare your threats.
    The bug which you would fright me with I seek.   90
    To me can life be no commodity.
    The crown and comfort of my life, your favour,
    I do give lost, for I do feel it gone,
    But know not how it went ; my second joy
    And first fruits of my body, from his presence   95
    I am barr'd, like one infectious ; my third comfort,
    Starr'd most unluckily, is from my breast—
    The innocent milk in it most innocent mouth—
    Hal'd out to murder ; myself on every post
    Proclaim'd a strumpet ; with immodest hatred   100
    The child-bed privilege denied, which 'longs
    To women of all fashion ; lastly, hurried
    Here to this place, i' th' open air, before
    I have got strength of limit. Now, my liege,
    Tell me what blessings I have here alive   105
    That I should fear to die. Therefore proceed.
    But yet hear this—mistake me not : no life,

I prize it not a straw, but for mine honour
Which I would free—if I shall be condemn'd
Upon surmises, all proofs sleeping else   110
But what your jealousies awake, I tell you
'Tis rigour, and not law.   Your honours all,
I do refer me to the oracle :
Apollo be my judge !
I LORD.   This your request
Is altogether just.   Therefore, bring forth,   115
And in Apollo's name, his oracle.   [*exeunt certain* OFFICERS.   The COURT OFFICIAL
HER.   The Emperor of Russia was my father ;   leaves.
O that he were alive, and here beholding
His daughter's trial ! that he did but see
The flatness of my misery ; yet with eyes   120
Of pity, not revenge !

            Re-enter OFFICERS, *with* CLEOMENES *and* DION.   The COURT OFFICIAL
                                                                     returns with
OFFI.   You here shall swear upon this sword of justice   CLEOMENES and
That you, Cleomenes and Dion, have   DION.
Been both at Delphos, and from thence have brought
This seal'd-up oracle, by the hand deliver'd   125
Of great Apollo's priest ; and that since then
You have not dar'd to break the holy seal
Nor read the secrets in't.
CLEO., DION.   All this we swear.
LEON. Break up the seals and read.   129
OFFI. [*reads.*]   ' Hermione is chaste ; Polixenes blameless ; Camillo
a true subject ; Leontes a jealous tyrant ; his innocent babe truly
begotten ; and the King shall live without an heir, if that which
is lost be not found.'
LORDS. Now blessed be the great Apollo !
HER.   Praised !
LEON. Hast thou read truth ?
OFFI.   Ay, my lord ; even so   135
As it is here set down.
LEON. There is no truth at all i' th' oracle.
The sessions shall proceed.   This is mere falsehood.

                        Enter a SERVANT.
SERV. My lord the King, the King !
LEON.   What is the business ?
SERV. O sir, I shall be hated to report it :   140
The Prince your son, with mere conceit and fear
Of the Queen's speed, is gone.
LEON.   How ! Gone ?
SERV.   Is dead.
LEON. Apollo's angry ; and the heavens themselves
Do strike at my injustice.   [HERMIONE *swoons*.
                        How now, there !
PAUL. This news is mortal to the Queen.   Look down   145
And see what death is doing.
LEON.   Take her hence.
Her heart is but o'ercharg'd ; she will recover.
I have too much believ'd mine own suspicion.

Beseech you tenderly apply to her
Some remedies for life.
                    [*exeunt* PAULINA *and* LADIES *with* HERMIONE.
                    Apollo, pardon   150
My great profaneness 'gainst thine oracle.
I'll reconcile me to Polixenes,
New woo my queen, recall the good Camillo—
Whom I proclaim a man of truth, of mercy.
For, being transported by my jealousies   155
To bloody thoughts and to revenge, I chose
Camillo for the minister to poison
My friend Polixenes ; which had been done
But that the good mind of Camillo tardied
My swift command, though I with death and with   160
Reward did threaten and encourage him,
Not doing it and being done. He, most humane
And fill'd with honour, to my kingly guest
Unclasp'd my practice, quit his fortunes here,
Which you knew great, and to the certain hazard   165
Of all incertainties himself commended,
No richer than his honour. How he glisters
Thorough my rust ! And how his piety
Does my deeds make the blacker !

                    Re-enter PAULINA.

PAUL.   Woe the while !
    O, cut my lace, lest my heart, cracking it,   170
    Break too !
1 LORD. What fit is this, good lady ?
PAUL. What studied torments, tyrant, hast for me ?
    What wheels, racks, fires ?   what flaying, boiling
    In leads or oils ?   What old or newer torture
    Must I receive, whose every word deserves   175
    To taste of thy most worst ?   Thy tyranny
    Together working with thy jealousies,
    Fancies too weak for boys, too green and idle
    For girls of nine—O, think what they have done,
    And then run mad indeed, stark mad ; for all   180
    Thy by-gone fooleries were but spices of it.
    That thou betray'dst Polixenes, 'twas nothing ;
    That did but show thee, of a fool, inconstant,
    And damnable ingrateful.   Nor was't much
    Thou wouldst have poison'd good Camillo's honour,   185
    To have him kill a king—poor trespasses,
    More monstrous standing by ; whereof I reckon
    The casting forth to crows thy baby daughter
    To be or none or little, though a devil
    Would have shed water out of fire ere done't ;   190
    Nor is't directly laid to thee, the death
    Of the young Prince, whose honourable thoughts—
    Thoughts high for one so tender—cleft the heart
    That could conceive a gross and foolish sire
    Blemish'd his gracious dam.   This is not, no,   195
    Laid to thy answer ; but the last—O lords,

When I have said, cry ' Woe ! '—the Queen, the Queen,
The sweet'st, dear'st creature's dead ; and vengeance for't
Not dropp'd down yet.
1 LORD.   The higher pow'rs forbid !   2 LORD.
PAUL. I say she's dead ; I'll swear't. If word nor oath   200
Prevail not, go and see. If you can bring
Tincture or lustre in her lip, her eye,
Heat outwardly or breath within, I'll serve you
As I would do the gods. But, O thou tyrant !
Do not repent these things, for they are heavier   205
Than all thy woes can stir ; therefore betake thee
To nothing but despair. A thousand knees
Ten thousand years together, naked, fasting,
Upon a barren mountain, and still winter
In storm perpetual, could not move the gods   210
To look that way thou wert.
LEON.   Go on, go on.
Thou canst not speak too much ; I have deserv'd
All tongues to talk their bitt'rest.
1 LORD.   Say no more ;   2 LORD.
Howe'er the business goes, you have made fault
I' th' boldness of your speech.
PAUL.   I am sorry for't.   215
All faults I make, when I shall come to know them,
I do repent. Alas, I have show'd too much
The rashness of a woman ! He is touch'd
To th' noble heart. What's gone and what's past help
Should be past grief. Do not receive affliction   220
At my petition ; I beseech you, rather
Let me be punish'd that have minded you
Of what you should forget. Now, good my liege,
Sir, royal sir, forgive a foolish woman.
The love I bore your queen—lo, fool again !   225
I'll speak of her no more, nor of your children ;
I'll not remember you of my own lord,
Who is lost too. Take your patience to you,
And I'll say nothing.
LEON.   Thou didst speak but well
When most the truth ; which I receive much better   230
Than to be pitied of thee. Prithee, bring me
To the dead bodies of my queen and son.
One grave shall be for both. Upon them shall
The causes of their death appear, unto
Our shame perpetual. Once a day I'll visit   235
The chapel where they lie ; and tears shed there
Shall be my recreation. So long as nature
Will bear up with this exercise, so long
I daily vow to use it. Come, and lead me
To these sorrows.   [exeunt.

SCENE III.   *Bohemia.   The sea-coast.*   SCENE 7
                                                        Exterior. Bohemia.
Enter ANTIGONUS *with the* CHILD, *and a* MARINER.   *Beach. Day.*
ANT. Thou art perfect then our ship hath touch'd upon

Cyril Luckham as Antigonus

The deserts of Bohemia ?
MAR.   Ay, my lord, and fear
  We have landed in ill time ; the skies look grimly
  And threaten present blusters. In my conscience,
  The heavens with that we have in hand are angry   5
  And frown upon 's.
ANT. Their sacred wills be done ! Go, get aboard ;
  Look to thy bark. I'll not be long before
  I call upon thee.
MAR. Make your best haste ; and go not
  Too far i' th' land ; 'tis like to be loud weather ;
  Besides, this place is famous for the creatures
  Of prey that keep upon't.
ANT.   Go thou away ;
  I'll follow instantly.
MAR.   I am glad at heart
  To be so rid o' th' business.   [exit.
ANT.   Come, poor babe.   15
  I have heard, but not believ'd, the spirits o' th' dead
  May walk again. If such thing be, thy mother
  Appear'd to me last night ; for ne'er was dream
  So like a waking. To me comes a creature,
  Sometimes her head on one side some another—   20
  I never saw a vessel of like sorrow,
  So fill'd and so becoming ; in pure white robes,
  Like very sanctity, she did approach
  My cabin where I lay ; thrice bow'd before me ;
  And, gasping to begin some speech, her eyes   25
  Became two spouts ; the fury spent, anon
  Did this break from her : ' Good Antigonus,
  Since fate, against thy better disposition,
  Hath made thy person for the thrower-out
  Of my poor babe, according to thine oath,   30
  Places remote enough are in Bohemia,
  There weep, and leave it crying ; and, for the babe
  Is counted lost for ever, Perdita
  I prithee call't. For this ungentle business,
  Put on thee by my lord, thou ne'er shalt see   35
  Thy wife Paulina more '. And so, with shrieks,
  She melted into air. Affrighted much,
  I did in time collect myself, and thought
  This was so and no slumber. Dreams are toys ;
  Yet, for this once, yea, superstitiously,   40
  I will be squar'd by this. I do believe
  Hermione hath suffer'd death, and that
  Apollo would, this being indeed the issue
  Of King Polixenes, it should here be laid,
  Either for life or death, upon the earth   45
  Of its right father. Blossom, speed thee well !
                      [laying down the child.
  There lie, and there thy character ; there these
                      [laying down a bundle.
  Which may, if fortune please, both breed thee, pretty,
  And still rest thine. The storm begins. Poor wretch,

That for thy mother's fault art thus expos'd   50
To loss and what may follow ! Weep I cannot,
But my heart bleeds ; and most accurs'd am I
To be by oath enjoin'd to this. Farewell !
The day frowns more and more. Thou'rt like to have
A lullaby too rough ; I never saw   55
The heavens so dim by day. [*noise of hunt within.*] A savage
    clamour !
Well may I get aboard ! This is the chase ;
I am gone for ever.   [*exit, pursued by a bear.*]

Enter an old SHEPHERD.

SCENE 8
*Exterior. Bohemia.
Beach. Day.
Some time later.*

SHEP. I would there were no age between ten and three and twenty,
    or that youth would sleep out the rest ; for there is nothing in
    the between but getting wenches with child, wronging the
    ancientry, stealing, fighting—[*horns.*] Hark you now ! Would
    any but these boil'd brains of nineteen and two and twenty hunt
    this weather ? They have scar'd away two of my best sheep,
    which I fear the wolf will sooner find than the master. If any
    where I have them, 'tis by the sea-side, browsing of ivy. Good
    luck, an't be thy will ! What have we here ? [*taking up the child.*]
    Mercy on's, a barne ! A very pretty barne. A boy or a child, I
    wonder ? A pretty one ; a very pretty one—sure, some scape.
    Though I am not bookish, yet I can read waiting-gentlewoman
    in the scape. This has been some stair-work, some trunk-work,
    some behind-door-work ; they were warmer that got this than
    the poor thing is here. I'll take it up for pity ; yet I'll tarry till
    my son come ; he halloo'd but even now. Whoa-ho-hoa ! 76

Enter CLOWN.

CLO. Hilloa, loa !
SHEP. What, art so near ? If thou'lt see a thing to talk on when
    thou art dead and rotten, come hither. What ail'st thou, man ?
CLO. I have seen two such sights, by sea and by land ! But I am not
    to say it is a sea, for it is now the sky ; betwixt the firmament and
    it you cannot thrust a bodkin's point.
SHEP. Why, boy, how is it ?   85
CLO. I would you did but see how it chafes, how it rages, how it takes
    up the shore ! But that's not to the point. O, the most piteous
    cry of the poor souls ! Sometimes to see 'em, and not to see 'em ;
    now the ship boring the moon with her mainmast, and anon
    swallowed with yeast and froth, as you'd thrust a cork into a hogs-
    head. And then for the land service—to see how the bear tore
    out his shoulder-bone ; how he cried to me for help, and said his
    name was Antigonus, a nobleman ! But to make an end of the
    ship—to see how the sea flap-dragon'd it ; but first, how the
    poor souls roared, and the sea mock'd them ; and how the poor
    gentleman roared, and the bear mock'd him, both roaring louder
    than the sea or weather.
SHEP. Name of mercy, when was this, boy ?   100
CLO. Now, now ; I have not wink'd since I saw these sights ; the
    men are not yet cold under water, nor the bear half din'd on the
    gentleman ; he's at it now.

Paul Jesson as the Clown and Arthur Hewlett as the Shepherd

SHEP. Would I had been by to have help'd the old man!
CLO. I would you had been by the ship-side, to have help'd her;
there your charity would have lack'd footing.
SHEP. Heavy matters, heavy matters! But look thee here, boy.
Now bless thyself; thou met'st with things dying, I with things
new-born. Here's a sight for thee; look thee, a bearing-cloth
for a squire's child! Look thee here; take up, take up, boy;
open't. So, let's see—it was told me I should be rich by the
fairies. This is some changeling. Open't. What's within, boy?
CLO. You're a made old man; if the sins of your youth are forgiven
you, you're well to live. Gold! all gold!   116
SHEP. This is fairy gold, boy, and 'twill prove so. Up with't, keep it
close. Home, home, the next way! We are lucky, boy; and
to be so still requires nothing but secrecy. Let my sheep go.
Come, good boy, the next way home.   121
CLO. Go you the next way with your findings. I'll go see if the bear
be gone from the gentleman, and how much he hath eaten. They
are never curst but when they are hungry. If there be any of him
left, I'll bury it.
SHEP. That's a good deed. If thou mayest discern by that which
is left of him what he is, fetch me to th' sight of him.
CLO. Marry, will I; and you shall help to put him i' th' ground. 130
SHEP. 'Tis a lucky day, boy; and we'll do good deeds on't.   [exeunt.

ACT FOUR.

SCENE I.

Enter TIME, *the* CHORUS.

TIME. I, that please some, try all, both joy and terror
Of good and bad, that makes and unfolds error,
Now take upon me, in the name of Time,
To use my wings. Impute it not a crime
To me or my swift passage that I slide   5
O'er sixteen years, and leave the growth untried
Of that wide gap, since it is in my pow'r
To o'erthrow law, and in one self-born hour
To plant and o'erwhelm custom. Let me pass
The same I am, ere ancient'st order was   10
Or what is now receiv'd. I witness to
The times that brought them in; so shall I do
To th' freshest things now reigning, and make stale
The glistering of this present, as my tale
Now seems to it. Your patience this allowing,   15
I turn my glass, and give my scene such growing
As you had slept between. Leontes leaving—
Th' effects of his fond jealousies so grieving
That he shuts up himself—imagine me,
Gentle spectators, that I now may be   20
In fair Bohemia; and remember well
I mention'd a son o' th' King's, which Florizel
I now name to you; and with speed so pace
To speak of Perdita, now grown in grace

Equal with wond'ring. What of her ensues   25
I list not prophesy ; but let Time's news
Be known when 'tis brought forth. A shepherd's daughter,
And what to her adheres, which follows after,
Is th' argument of Time. Of this allow,
If ever you have spent time worse ere now ;   30
If never, yet that Time himself doth say
He wishes earnestly you never may.   [*exit.*

SCENE II. *Bohemia. The palace of Polixenes.*

Enter POLIXENES *and* CAMILLO.

SCENE 10
Exterior. Bohemia.
Beach. Day.

POL. I pray thee, good Camillo, be no more importunate : 'tis a
sickness denying thee anything ; a death to grant this.

CAM. It is fifteen years since I saw my country ; though I have for
the most part been aired abroad, I desire to lay my bones there.
Besides, the penitent King, my master, hath sent for me ; to
whose feeling sorrows I might be some allay, or I o'erween to
think so, which is another spur to my departure.   9

POL. As thou lov'st me, Camillo, wipe not out the rest of thy services
by leaving me now. The need I have of thee thine own goodness
hath made. Better not to have had thee than thus to want thee ;
thou, having made me businesses which none without thee can
sufficiently manage, must either stay to execute them thyself, or
take away with thee the very services thou hast done ; which if I
have not enough considered—as too much I cannot—to be more
thankful to thee shall be my study ; and my profit therein the
heaping friendships. Of that fatal country Sicilia, prithee,
speak no more ; whose very naming punishes me with the
remembrance of that penitent, as thou call'st him, and reconciled
king, my brother ; whose loss of his most precious queen and
children are even now to be afresh lamented. Say to me, when
saw'st thou the Prince Florizel, my son ? Kings are no less
unhappy, their issue not being gracious, than they are in losing
them when they have approved their virtues.   27

'which if I . . .
heaping friendships'
omitted.

CAM. Sir, it is three days since I saw the Prince. What his happier
affairs may be are to me unknown ; but I have missingly noted
he is of late much retired from court, and is less frequent to his
princely exercises than formerly he hath appeared.   32

POL. I have considered so much, Camillo, and with some care, so far
that I have eyes under my service which look upon his removedness ; from whom I have this intelligence, that he is seldom from
the house of a most homely shepherd—a man, they say, that from
very nothing, and beyond the imagination of his neighbours, is
grown into an unspeakable estate.   39

CAM. I have heard, sir, of such a man, who hath a daughter of most
rare note. The report of her is extended more than can be thought
to begin from such a cottage.

POL. That's likewise part of my intelligence ; but, I fear, the angle
that plucks our son thither. Thou shalt accompany us to the
place ; where we will, not appearing what we are, have some
question with the shepherd ; from whose simplicity I think it not
uneasy to get the cause of my son's resort thither. Prithee be my

67

present partner in this business, and lay aside the thoughts of
Sicilia.
CAM. I willingly obey your command.   50
POL. My best Camillo! We must disguise ourselves.   [*exeunt.*

SCENE III. *Bohemia.   A road near the shepherd's cottage.*

Enter AUTOLYCUS, *singing.*

SCENE 11
*Exterior. Bohemia.
Countryside. Day.*

When daffodils begin to peer,
   With heigh! the doxy over the dale,
Why, then comes in the sweet o' the year,
   For the red blood reigns in the winter's pale.

The white sheet bleaching on the hedge,   5
   With heigh! the sweet birds, O, how they sing!
Doth set my pugging tooth on edge,
   For a quart of ale is a dish for a king.

The lark, that tirra-lirra chants,
   With heigh! with heigh! the thrush and the jay, 10
Are summer songs for me and my aunts,
   While we lie tumbling in the hay.

I have serv'd Prince Florizel, and in my time wore three-pile;
but now I am out of service.

But shall I go mourn for that, my dear?   15
   The pale moon shines by night;
And when I wander here and there,
   I then do most go right.

If tinkers may have leave to live,
   And bear the sow-skin budget,   20
Then my account I well may give
   And in the stocks avouch it.

My traffic is sheets; when the kite builds, look to lesser linen.
My father nam'd me Autolycus; who, being, as I am, litter'd
under Mercury, was likewise a snapper-up of unconsidered trifles.
With die and drab I purchas'd this caparison; and my revenue
is the silly-cheat. Gallows and knock are too powerful on the
highway; beating and hanging are terrors to me; for the life to
come, I sleep out the thought of it. A prize! a prize!   30

Enter CLOWN.

CLO. Let me see: every 'leven wether tods; every tod yields pound
   and odd shilling; fifteen hundred shorn, what comes the wool to?
AUT. [*aside.*] If the springe hold, the cock's mine.
CLO. I cannot do 't without counters. Let me see: what am I to
   buy for our sheep-shearing feast? Three pound of sugar, five
   pound of currants, rice—what will this sister of mine do with rice?
   But my father hath made her mistress of the feast, and she lays
   it on. She hath made me four and twenty nosegays for the
   shearers—three-man song-men all, and very good ones; but

they are most of them means and bases ; but one Puritan amongst
them, and he sings psalms to hornpipes.   I must have saffron to
colour the warden pies ; mace ; dates—none, that's out of my
note ; nutmegs, seven ; a race or two of ginger, but that I may
beg ; four pound of prunes, and as many of raisins o' th' sun.

AUT. [*grovelling on the ground.*]   O that ever I was born !

CLO. I' th' name of me !

AUT. O, help me, help me !   Pluck but off these rags ; and then,
death, death !   50

CLO. Alack, poor soul !   thou hast need of more rags to lay on thee,
rather than have these off.

AUT. O sir, the loathsomeness of them offend me more than the
stripes I have received, which are mighty ones and millions.

CLO. Alas, poor man !   a million of beating may come to a great
matter.

AUT. I am robb'd, sir, and beaten ; my money and apparel ta'en
from me, and these detestable things put upon me.   60

CLO. What, by a horseman or a footman ?

AUT. A footman, sweet sir, a footman.

CLO. Indeed, he should be a footman, by the garments he has left
with thee ; if this be a horseman's coat, it hath seen very hot
service.   Lend me thy hand, I'll help thee.   Come, lend me thy
hand.   [*helping him up.*]

AUT. O, good sir, tenderly, O !

CLO. Alas, poor soul !

AUT. O, good sir, softly, good sir ; I fear, sir, my shoulder blade is
out.   70

CLO. How now !   Canst stand ?

AUT. Softly, dear sir [*picks his pocket*] ; good sir, softly.   You ha'
done me a charitable office.

CLO. Dost lack any money ?   I have a little money for thee.

AUT. No, good sweet sir ; no, I beseech you, sir.   I have a kinsman
not past three quarters of a mile hence, unto whom I was going ;
I shall there have money or anything I want.   Offer me no money,
I pray you ; that kills my heart.   80

CLO. What manner of fellow was he that robb'd you ?

AUT. A fellow, sir, that I have known to go about with troll-my-
dames ; I knew him once a servant of the Prince.   I cannot tell,
good sir, for which of his virtues it was, but he was certainly
whipt out of the court.   85

CLO. His vices, you would say ; there's no virtue whipt out of the
court.   They cherish it to make it stay there ; and yet it will
no more but abide.

AUT. Vices, I would say, sir.   I know this man well ; he hath been
since an ape-bearer ; then a process-server, a bailiff ; then he
compass'd a motion of the Prodigal Son, and married a tinker's
wife within a mile where my land and living lies ; and, having
flown over many knavish professions, he settled only in rogue.
Some call him Autolycus.   95

CLO. Out upon him !   prig, for my life, prig !   He haunts wakes,
fairs, and bear-baitings.

AUT. Very true, sir ; he, sir, he ; that's the rogue that put me into
this apparel.

CLO. Not a more cowardly rogue in all Bohemia ; if you had but
look'd big and spit at him, he'd have run.
AUT. I must confess to you, sir, I am no fighter ; I am false of heart
that way ; and that he knew, I warrant him.
CLO. How do you now ?   105
AUT. Sweet sir, much better than I was ; I can stand and walk.   I
will even take my leave of you and pace softly towards my
kinsman's.
CLO. Shall I bring thee on the way ?
AUT. No, good-fac'd sir ; no, sweet sir.
CLO. Then fare thee well.   I must go buy spices for our sheep-
shearing.   112
AUT. Prosper you, sweet sir !   [exit CLOWN.
Your purse is not hot enough to purchase your spice.   I'll be
with you at your sheep-shearing too.   If I make not this cheat
bring out another, and the shearers prove sheep, let me be unroll'd,
and my name put in the book of virtue !   [sings.
            Jog on, jog on, the footpath way,
            And merrily hent the stile-a ;
            A merry heart goes all the day,   120
            Your sad tires in a mile-a.   [exit

SCENE IV.   Bohemia.   The Shepherd's cottage.

Enter FLORIZEL and PERDITA.

FLO. These your unusual weeds to each part of you
Do give a life—no shepherdess, but Flora
Peering in April's front.   This your sheep-shearing
Is as a meeting of the petty gods,
And you the Queen on't.
PER.   Sir, my gracious lord,   5
To chide at your extremes it not becomes me—
O, pardon that I name them !   Your high self,
The gracious mark o' th' land, you have obscur'd
With a swain's wearing ; and me, poor lowly maid,
Most goddess-like prank'd up.   But that our feasts   10
In every mess have folly, and the feeders
Digest it with a custom, I should blush
To see you so attir'd ; swoon, I think,
To show myself a glass.
FLO.   I bless the time
When my good falcon made her flight across   15
Thy father's ground.
PER.   Now Jove afford you cause !
To me the difference forges dread ; your greatness
Hath not been us'd to fear.   Even now I tremble
To think your father, by some accident,
Should pass this way, as you did.   O, the Fates   20
How would he look to see his work, so noble,
Vilely bound up ?   What would he say ?   Or how
Should I, in these my borrow'd flaunts, behold
The sternness of his presence ?
FLO.   Apprehend
Nothing but jollity.   The gods themselves,   25

SCENE 12
Exterior. Bohemia.
Countryside. Day.

70

  Humbling their deities to love, have taken
  The shapes of beasts upon them : Jupiter
  Became a bull and bellow'd ; the green Neptune
  A ram and bleated ; and the fire-rob'd god,
  Golden Apollo, a poor humble swain,   30
  As I seem now. Their transformations
  Were never for a piece of beauty rarer,
  Nor in a way so chaste, since my desires
  Run not before mine honour, nor my lusts
  Burn hotter than my faith.
PER.   O, but, sir,   35
  Your resolution cannot hold when 'tis
  Oppos'd, as it must be, by th' pow'r of the King.
  One of these two must be necessities,
  Which then will speak, that you must change this purpose,
  Or I my life.
FLO.   Thou dearest Perdita,   40
  With these forc'd thoughts, I prithee, darken not
  The mirth o' th' feast. Or I'll be thine, my fair,
  Or not my father's ; for I cannot be
  Mine own, nor anything to any, if
  I be not thine. To this I am most constant,   45
  Though destiny say no. Be merry, gentle ;
  Strangle such thoughts as these with any thing
  That you behold the while. Your guests are coming.
  Lift up your countenance, as it were the day
  Of celebration of that nuptial which   50
  We two have sworn shall come.
PER.   O Lady Fortune,
  Stand you auspicious !
FLO.   See, your guests approach.
  Address yourself to entertain them sprightly,
  And let's be red with mirth.

Enter SHEPHERD, *with* POLIXENES *and* CAMILLO, *disguised ;* CLOWN,
    MOPSA, DORCAS, *with* OTHERS.

SHEP. Fie, daughter ! When my old wife liv'd, upon 55
  This day she was both pantler, butler, cook ;
  Both dame and servant ; welcom'd all ; serv'd all ;
  Would sing her song and dance her turn ; now here
  At upper end o' th' table, now i' th' middle ;
  On his shoulder, and his ; her face o' fire   60
  With labour, and the thing she took to quench it
  She would to each one sip. You are retired,
  As if you were a feasted one, and not
  The hostess of the meeting. Pray you bid
  These unknown friends to's welcome, for it is 65
  A way to make us better friends, more known.
  Come, quench your blushes, and present yourself
  That which you are, Mistress o' th' Feast. Come on,
  And bid us welcome to your sheep-shearing,
  As your good flock shall prosper.
PER. [*to* POLIXENES.]   Sir, welcome.   70
  It is my father's will I should take on me

The hostess-ship o' th' day. [*to* CAMILLO.]
You're welcome, sir.
Give me those flow'rs there, Dorcas.   Reverend sirs,
For you there's rosemary and rue ; these keep
Seeming and savour all the winter long.   75
Grace and remembrance be to you both !
And welcome to our shearing.
POL.   Shepherdess—
A fair one are you—well you fit our ages
With flow'rs of winter.
PER.   Sir, the year growing ancient,
Not yet on summer's death nor on the birth   80
Of trembling winter, the fairest flow'rs o' th' season
Are our carnations and streak'd gillyvors,
Which some call nature's bastards.   Of that kind
Our rustic garden's barren ; and I care not
To get slips of them.
POL.   Wherefore, gentle maiden,   85
Do you neglect them ?
PER.   For I have heard it said
There is an art which in their piedness shares
With great creating nature.
POL.   Say there be ;
Yet nature is made better by no mean
But nature makes that mean ; so over that art   90
Which you say adds to nature, is an art
That nature makes.   You see, sweet maid, we marry
A gentler scion to the wildest stock,
And make conceive a bark of baser kind
By bud of nobler race.   This is an art   95
Which does mend nature—change it rather ; but
The art itself is nature.
PER.   So it is.
POL. Then make your garden rich in gillyvors,
And do not call them bastards.
PER.   I'll not put
The dibble in earth to set one slip of them ;   100
No more than were I painted I would wish
This youth should say 'twere well, and only therefore
Desire to breed by me.   Here's flow'rs for you :
Hot lavender, mints, savory, marjoram ;
The marigold, that goes to bed wi' th' sun,   105
And with him rises weeping ; these are flow'rs
Of middle summer, and I think they are given
To men of middle age.   Y'are very welcome.
CAM. I should leave grazing, were I of your flock,
And only live by gazing.
PER.   Out, alas !   110
You'd be so lean that blasts of January
Would blow you through and through.   Now, my fair'st friend,
I would I had some flow'rs o' th' spring that might
Become your time of day—and yours, and yours,
That wear upon your virgin branches yet   115
Your maidenheads growing.   O Proserpina,

For the flowers now that, frighted, thou let'st fall
From Dis's waggon !—daffodils,
That come before the swallow dares, and take
The winds of March with beauty ; violets, dim   120
But sweeter than the lids of Juno's eyes
Or Cytherea's breath ; pale primroses,
That die unmarried ere they can behold
Bright Phœbus in his strength—a malady
Most incident to maids ; bold oxlips, and   125
The crown-imperial ; lilies of all kinds,
The flow'r-de-luce being one. O, these I lack
To make you garlands of, and my sweet friend
To strew him o'er and o'er !
FLO.   What, like a corse ?
PER. No ; like a bank for love to lie and play on ;   130
Not like a corse ; or if—not to be buried,
But quick, and in mine arms. Come, take your flow'rs.
Methinks I play as I have seen them do
In Whitsun pastorals. Sure, this robe of mine
Does change my disposition.
FLO.   What you do   135
Still betters what is done. When you speak, sweet,
I'd have you do it ever. When you sing,
I'd have you buy and sell so ; so give alms ;
Pray so ; and, for the ord'ring your affairs,
To sing them too. When you do dance, I wish you   140
A wave o' th' sea, that you might ever do
Nothing but that ; move still, still so,
And own no other function. Each your doing,
So singular in each particular,
Crowns what you are doing in the present deeds,   145
That all your acts are queens.
PER.   O Doricles,
Your praises are too large. But that your youth,
And the true blood which peeps fairly through't,
Do plainly give you out an unstain'd shepherd,
With wisdom I might fear, my Doricles,   150
You woo'd me the false way.
FLO.   I think you have
As little skill to fear as I have purpose
To put you to't. But, come ; our dance, I pray.
Your hand, my Perdita ; so turtles pair
That never mean to part.
PER.   I'll swear for 'em.   155
POL. This is the prettiest low-born lass that ever
Ran on the green-sward ; nothing she does or seems
But smacks of something greater than herself,
Too noble for this place.
CAM.   He tells her something
That makes her blood look out. Good sooth, she is   160
The queen of curds and cream.
CLO.   Come on, strike up.
DOR. Mopsa must be your mistress ; marry, garlic,
To mend her kissing with !

MOP.   Now, in good time !
CLO. Not a word, a word ; we stand upon our manners.
Come, strike up.
                                     [*music.*

     Here a dance of SHEPHERDS *and* SHEPHERDESSES.

POL. Pray, good shepherd, what fair swain is this   166
   Which dances with your daughter ?
SHEP. They call him Doricles, and boasts himself
   To have a worthy feeding ; but I have it
   Upon his own report, and I believe it :   170
   He looks like sooth. He says he loves my daughter ;
   I think so too ; for never gaz'd the moon
   Upon the water as he'll stand and read
   As 'twere my daughter's eyes ; and, to be plain,
   I think there is not half a kiss to choose   175
   Who loves another best.
POL.   She dances featly.
SHEP. So she does any thing ; though I report it
   That should be silent. If young Doricles
   Do light upon her, she shall bring him that
   Which he not dreams of.   180

            Enter a SERVANT.

SERV. O master, if you did but hear the pedlar at the door, you
   would never dance again after a tabor and pipe ; no, the bagpipe
   could not move you. He sings several tunes faster than you'll
   tell money ; he utters them as he had eaten ballads, and all men's
   ears grew to his tunes.   185
CLO. He could never come better ; he shall come in. I love a
   ballad but even too well, if it be doleful matter merrily set down,
   or a very pleasant thing indeed and sung lamentably.
SERV. He hath songs for man or woman of all sizes ; no milliner can
   so fit his customers with gloves. He has the prettiest love-songs
   for maids ; so without bawdry, which is strange ; with such
   delicate burdens of dildos and fadings, ' jump her and thump
   her ' ; and where some stretch-mouth'd rascal would, as it were,
   mean mischief, and break a foul gap into the matter, he makes
   the maid to answer ' Whoop, do me no harm, good man '—puts
   him off, slights him, with ' Whoop, do me no harm, good man '.
POL. This is a brave fellow.   199
CLO. Believe me, thou talkest of an admirable conceited fellow. Has
   he any unbraided wares ?
SERV. He hath ribbons of all the colours i' th' rainbow ; points,
   more than all the lawyers in Bohemia can learnedly handle,
   though they come to him by th' gross ; inkles, caddisses, cambrics,
   lawns. Why he sings 'em over as they were gods or goddesses ;
   you would think a smock were a she-angel, he so chants to the
   sleeve-hand and the work about the square on't.   208
CLO. Prithee bring him in ; and let him approach singing.
PER. Forewarn him that he use no scurrilous words in's tunes.
                                [*exit* SERVANT.
CLO. You have of these pedlars that have more in them than you'd
   think, sister.
PER. Ay, good brother, or go about to think.

Enter AUTOLYCUS, *singing* ♪

Lawn as white as driven snow ;   215
Cypress black as e'er was crow ;
Gloves as sweet as damask roses ;
Masks for faces and for noses ;
Bugle bracelet, necklace amber,
Perfume for a lady's chamber ;   220
Golden quoifs and stomachers,
For my lads to give their dears ;
Pins and poking-sticks of steel—
What maids lack from head to heel.
Come, buy of me, come ; come buy, come buy ; 225
Buy, lads, or else your lasses cry.
Come, buy.

CLO. If I were not in love with Mopsa, thou shouldst take no money
of me ; but being enthrall'd as I am, it will also be the bondage of
certain ribbons and gloves.   230
MOP. I was promis'd them against the feast ; but they come not too
late now.
DOR. He hath promis'd you more than that, or there be liars.
MOP. He hath paid you all he promis'd you. May be he has paid
you more, which will shame you to give him again.   237
CLO. Is there no manners left among maids ? Will they wear their
plackets where they should bear their faces ? Is there not
milking-time, when you are going to bed, or kiln-hole, to whistle
off these secrets, but you must be tittle-tattling before all our
guests ? 'Tis well they are whisp'ring. Clammer your tongues,
and not a word more.
MOP. I have done. Come, you promis'd me a tawdry-lace, and a
pair of sweet gloves.   245
CLO. Have I not told thee how I was cozen'd by the way, and lost
all my money ?
AUT. And indeed, sir, there are cozeners abroad ; therefore it behoves
men to be wary.
CLO. Fear not thou, man ; thou shalt lose nothing here.
AUT. I hope so, sir ; for I have about me many parcels of charge.
CLO. What hast here ? Ballads ?
MOP. Pray now, buy some. I love a ballad in print a-life, for then
we are sure they are true.   255
AUT. Here's one to a very doleful tune : how a usurer's wife was
brought to bed of twenty money-bags at a burden, and how she
long'd to eat adders' heads and toads carbonado'd.
MOP. Is it true, think you ?
AUT. Very true, and but a month old.
DOR. Bless me from marrying a usurer !
AUT. Here's the midwife's name to't, one Mistress Taleporter, and
five or six honest wives that were present. Why should I carry
lies abroad ?   265
MOP. Pray you now, buy it.
CLO. Come on, lay it by ; and let's first see moe ballads ; we'll buy
the other things anon.
AUT. Here's another ballad, of a fish that appeared upon the coast on

Wednesday the fourscore of April, forty thousand fathom above
water, and sung this ballad against the hard hearts of maids. It
was thought she was a woman, and was turn'd into a cold fish for
she would not exchange flesh with one that lov'd her. The
ballad is very pitiful, and as true.   275
DOR. Is it true too, think you?
AUT. Five justices' hands at it; and witnesses more than my pack
    will hold.
CLO. Lay it by too. Another.
AUT. This is a merry ballad, but a very pretty one.
MOP. Let's have some merry ones.
AUT. Why, this is a passing merry one, and goes to the tune of ' Two
    maids wooing a man '. There's scarce a maid westward but she
    sings it; 'tis in request, I can tell you.   285
MOP. We can both sing it. If thou'lt bear a part, thou shalt hear;
    'tis in three parts.
DOR. We had the tune on't a month ago.
AUT. I can bear my part; you must know 'tis my occupation. Have
    at it with you.   290

                              Song

AUT.   Get you hence, for I must go
            Where it fits not you to know.
DOR.   Whither?
MOP.   O, whither?
DOR.   Whither?
MOP.   It becomes thy oath full well
            Thou to me thy secrets tell.   295
DOR.   Me too! Let me go thither
MOP.   Or thou goest to th' grange or mill.
DOR.   If to either, thou dost ill.
AUT.   Neither.
DOR.   What, neither?
AUT.   Neither.
DOR.   Thou has sworn my love to be.   300
MOP.   Thou hast sworn it more to me
            Then whither goest?   Say, whither?

CLO. We'll have this song out anon by ourselves; my father and the
    gentlemen are in sad talk, and we'll not trouble them. Come,
    bring away thy pack after me. Wenches, I'll buy for you both.
    Pedlar, let's have the first choice. Follow me, girls.
                              [*exit with* DORCAS *and* MOPSA.
AUT. And you shal. pay well for 'em.   [*exit* AUTOLYCUS, *singing :*
            Wil you buy any tape,
            Or lace for your cape,
            My dainty duck, my dear-a?   310
            Any silk, any thread,
            Any toys for your head,
            Of the new'st and fin'st, fin'st wear-a?
            Come to the pedlar;
            Money's a meddler   315
            That doth utter all men's ware-a.

The assembled
company, apart from
POLIXENES, CAMILLO,
PERDITA, FLORIZEL
and the SHEPHERD,
leave with
AUTOLYCUS.

Re-enter SERVANT.

SERV. Master, there is three carters, three shepherds, three neat-herds,
    three swineherds, that have made themselves all men of hair;
    they call themselves Saltiers, and they have a dance which the
    wenches say is a gallimaufry of gambols, because they are not in't;
    but they themselves are o' th' mind, if it be not too rough for some
    that know little but bowling, it will please plentifully.   324

SHEP. Away! We'll none on't; here has been too much homely
    foolery already. I know, sir, we weary you.

POL. You weary those that refresh us. Pray, let's see these four
    threes of herdsmen.

SERV. One three of them, by their own report, sir, hath danc'd before
    the King; and not the worst of the three but jumps twelve foot
    and a half by th' squier.   331

SHEP. Leave your prating; since these good men are pleas'd, let
    them come in; but quickly now.

SERV. Why, they stay at door, sir.   [*exit*.

Here a Dance of twelve Satyrs.

POL. [*to* SHEPHERD.]   O, father, you'll know more of that hereafter.
    [*to* CAMILLO.] Is it not too far gone? 'Tis time to part them.
    He's simple and tells much. [*to Florizel.*] How now, fair shepherd!
    Your heart is full of something that does take
    Your mind from feasting. Sooth, when I was young
    And handed love as you do, I was wont   340
    To load my she with knacks; I would have ransack'd
    The pedlar's silken treasury and have pour'd it
    To her acceptance: you have let him go
    And nothing marted with him. If your lass
    Interpretation should abuse and call this   345
    Your lack of love or bounty, you were straited
    For a reply, at least if you make a care
    Of happy holding her.

FLO.   Old sir, I know
    She prizes not such trifles as these are.
    The gifts she looks from me are pack'd and lock'd   350
    Up in my heart, which I have given already,
    But not deliver'd. O, hear me breathe my life
    Before this ancient sir, whom, it should seem,
    Hath sometime lov'd. I take thy hand—this hand,
    As soft as dove's down and as white as it,   355
    Or Ethiopian's tooth, or the fann'd snow that's bolted
    By th' northern blasts twice o'er.

POL.   What follows this?
    How prettily the young swain seems to wash
    The hand was fair before! I have put you out.
    But to your protestation; let me hear   360
    What you profess.

FLO.   Do, and be witness to't.

POL. And this my neighbour too?

FLO.   And he, and more
    Than he, and men—the earth, the heavens, and all:
    That, were I crown'd the most imperial monarch,

Lines 318–335,
'Master, there . . .
that hereafter',
omitted.

Thereof most worthy, were I the fairest youth   365
That ever made eye swerve, had force and knowledge
More than was ever man's, I would not prize them
Without her love ; for her employ them all ;
Commend them and condemn them to her service
Or to their own perdition.
POL.   Fairly offer'd.   370
CAM. This shows a sound affection.
SHEP.   But, my daughter,
Say you the like to him ?
PER.   I cannot speak
So well, nothing so well ; no, nor mean better.
By th' pattern of mine own thoughts I cut out
The purity of his.
SHEP.   Take hands, a bargain !   375
And, friends unknown, you shall bear witness to't :
I give my daughter to him, and will make
Her portion equal his.
FLO.   O, that must be
I' th' virtue of your daughter.   One being dead,
I shall have more than you can dream of yet ;   380
Enough then for your wonder.   But come on,
Contract us fore these witnesses.
SHEP.   Come, your hand ;
And, daughter, yours.
POL. Soft, swain, awhile, beseech you ; Have you a father ?
FLO.   I have, but what of him ?
POL. Knows he of this ?
FLO.   He neither does nor shall.   385
POL. Methinks a father
Is at the nuptial of his son a guest
That best becomes the table.   Pray you, once more,
Is not your father grown incapable
Of reasonable affairs ?   Is he not stupid   390
With age and alt'ring rheums ?   Can he speak, hear,
Know man from man, dispute his own estate ?
Lies he not bed-rid, and again does nothing
But what he did being childish ?
FLO.   No, good sir ;
He has his health, and ampler strength indeed
Than most have of his age.   395
POL.   By my white beard,
You offer him, if this be so, a wrong
Something unfilial.   Reason my son
Should choose himself a wife ; but as good reason
The father—all whose joy is nothing else
But fair posterity—should hold some counsel   400
In such a business.
FLO.   I yield all this ;
But, for some other reasons, my grave sir,
Which 'tis not fit you know, I not acquaint
My father of this business.
POL.   Let him know't.
FLO. He shall not.   405

Lines 386–396,
'. . . his age', omitted.

POL.   Prithee let him.
FLO.   No, he must not.
SHEP. Let him, my son ; he shall not need to grieve
     At knowing of thy choice.
FLO.   Come, come, he must not.
     Mark our contract.
POL. [*discovering himself.*] Mark your divorce, young sir,
     Whom son I dare not call ; thou art too base   410
     To be acknowledg'd—thou a sceptre's heir,
     That thus affects a sheep-hook ! Thou, old traitor,
     I am sorry that by hanging thee I can but
     Shorten thy life one week. And thou, fresh piece
     Of excellent witchcraft, who of force must know   415
     The royal fool thou cop'st with—
SHEP.   O, my heart !
POL. I'll have thy beauty scratch'd with briers and made
     More homely than thy state. For thee, fond boy,
     If I may ever know thou dost but sigh
     That thou no more shalt see this knack—as never   420
     I mean thou shalt—we'll bar thee from succession ;
     Not hold thee of our blood, no, not our kin,
     Farre than Deucalion off. Mark thou my words.
     Follow us to the court. Thou churl, for this time,
     Though full of our displeasure, yet we free thee   425
     From the dead blow of it. And you, enchantment,
     Worthy enough a herdsman—yea, him too
     That makes himself, but for our honour therein,
     Unworthy thee—if ever henceforth thou
     These rural latches to his entrance open,   430
     Or hoop his body more with thy embraces,
     I will devise a death as cruel for thee
     As thou art tender to't.   [*exit.*
PER.   Even here undone !
     I was not much afeard ; for once or twice
     I was about to speak and tell him plainly   435
     The self-same sun that shines upon his court
     Hides not his visage from our cottage, but
     Looks on alike. [*to Florizel.*] Will't please you, sir, be gone ?
     I told you what would come of this. Beseech you,
     Of your own state take care. This dream of mine—   440
     Being now awake, I'll queen it no inch farther,
     But milk my ewes and weep.
CAM.   Why, how now, father !
     Speak ere thou diest.
SHEP.   I cannot speak nor think,
     Nor dare to know that which I know. [*to* FLORIZEL.] O sir,
     You have undone a man of fourscore-three   445
     That thought to fill his grave in quiet, yea,
     To die upon the bed my father died,
     To lie close by his honest bones ; but now
     Some hangman must put on my shroud and lay me
     Where no priest shovels in dust. [*to* PERDITA.] O cursed wretch,
     That knew'st this was the Prince, and wouldst adventure
     To mingle faith with him !—Undone, undone !

If I might die within this hour, I have liv'd
To die when I desire.
FLO.   Why look you so upon me ?   [*exit.*
I am but sorry, not afeard ; delay'd,   455
But nothing alt'red.   What I was, I am :
More straining on for plucking back ; not following
My leash unwillingly.
CAM.   Gracious my lord,
You know your father's temper.   At this time
He will allow no speech—which I do guess   460
You do not purpose to him—and as hardly
Will he endure your sight as yet, I fear ;
Then, till the fury of his Highness settle,
Come not before him.
FLO.   I not purpose it.
I think Camillo ?
CAM.   Even he, my lord.   465
PER. How often have I told you 'twould be thus !
How often said my dignity would last
But till 'twere known !
FLO.   It cannot fail but by
The violation of my faith ; and then
Let nature crush the sides o' th' earth together   470
And mar the seeds within ! Lift up thy looks.
From my succession wipe me, father ; I
Am heir to my affection.
CAM.   Be advis'd.
FLO. I am—and by my fancy ; if my reason
Will thereto be obedient, I have reason ;   475
If not, my senses, better pleas'd with madness,
Do bid it welcome.
CAM.   This is desperate, sir.
FLO. So call it ; but it does fulfil my vow :
I needs must think it honesty.   Camillo,
Not for Bohemia, nor the pomp that may   480
Be thereat glean'd, for all the sun sees or
The close earth wombs, or the profound seas hides
In unknown fathoms, will I break my oath
To this my fair belov'd.   Therefore, I pray you,
As you have ever been my father's honour'd friend,   485
When he shall miss me—as, in faith, I mean not
To see him any more—cast your good counsels
Upon his passion.   Let myself and Fortune
Tug for the time to come.   This you may know,
And so deliver : I am put to sea   490
With her who here I cannot hold on shore.
And most opportune to her need I have
A vessel rides fast by, but not prepar'd
For this design.   What course I mean to hold
Shall nothing benefit your knowledge, nor   495
Concern me the reporting.
CAM.   O my lord,
I would your spirit were easier for advice,
Or stronger for your need.

Jeremy Kemp as Leontes and Anna Calder-Marshall as Hermoine in the trial scene

Jeremy Kemp as Leontes

*Paulina (Margaret Tyzack) and Antigonus (Cyril Luckham) with Leontes
(Jeremy Kemp)*

Debbie Farrington as Perdita and Robin Kermode as Florizel

Paul Jesson as the Clown and Rikki Fulton as Autolycus

Robert Stephens as Polixenes and David Burke as Camillo

*Leontes (Jeremy Kemp) and Hermione (Anna Calder-Marshall) with Perdita
(Debbie Farrington)*

FLO.   Hark, Perdita.   [*takes her aside.*
  [*to Camillo.*]   I'll hear you by and by.
CAM.   He's irremovable,
  Resolv'd for flight.   Now were I happy if   500
  His going I could frame to serve my turn,
  Save him from danger, do him love and honour,
  Purchase the sight again of dear Sicilia
  And that unhappy king, my master, whom
  I so much thirst to see.
FLO.   Now, good Camillo,   505
  I am so fraught with curious business that
  I leave out ceremony.
CAM.   Sir, I think
  You have heard of my poor services i' th' love
  That I have borne your father ?
FLO.   Very nobly
  Have you deserv'd.   It is my father's music   510
  To speak your deeds ; not little of his care
  To have them recompens'd as thought on.
CAM.   Well, my lord,
  If you may please to think I love the King,
  And through him what's nearest to him, which is
  Your gracious self, embrace but my direction.   515
  If your more ponderous and settled project
  May suffer alteration, on mine honour,
  I'll point you where you shall have such receiving
  As shall become your Highness ; where you may
  Enjoy your mistress, from the whom, I see,   520
  There's no disjunction to be made but by,
  As heavens forfend ! your ruin—marry her ;
  And with my best endeavours in your absence
  Your discontenting father strive to qualify,
  And bring him up to liking.
FLO.   How, Camillo,   525
  May this, almost a miracle, be done ?
  That I may call thee something more than man,
  And after that trust to thee.
CAM.   Have you thought on
  A place whereto you'll go ?
FLO.   Not any yet ;
  But as th' unthought-on accident is guilty   530
  To what we wildly do, so we profess
  Ourselves to be the slaves of chance and flies
  Of every wind that blows.
CAM.   Then list to me.
  This follows, if you will not change your purpose
  But undergo this flight : make for Sicilia,   535
  And there present yourself and your fair princess—
  For so, I see, she must be—fore Leontes.
  She shall be habited as it becomes
  The partner of your bed.   Methinks I see
  Leontes opening his free arms and weeping   540
  His welcomes forth ; asks thee there ' Son, forgiveness ! '
  As 'twere i' th' father's person ; kisses the hands

Of your fresh princess ; o'er and o'er divides him
'Twixt his unkindness and his kindness—th'one
He chides to hell, and bids the other grow   545
Faster than thought or time.
FLO.   Worthy Camillo,
What colour for my visitation shall I
Hold up before him ?
CAM.   Sent by the King your father
To greet him and to give him comforts.   Sir,
The manner of your bearing towards him, with   550
What you as from your father shall deliver,
Things known betwixt us three, I'll write you down ;
The which shall point you forth at every sitting
What you must say, that he shall not perceive
But that you have your father's bosom there   555
And speak his very heart.
FLO.   I am bound to you.
There is some sap in this.
CAM.   A course more promising
Than a wild dedication of yourselves
To unpath'd waters, undream'd shores, most certain
To miseries enough ; no hope to help you,   560
But as you shake off one to take another ;
Nothing so certain as your anchors, who
Do their best office if they can but stay you
Where you'll be loath to be.   Besides, you know
Prosperity's the very bond of love,   565
Whose fresh complexion and whose heart together
Affliction alters.
PER.   One of these is true :
I think affliction may subdue the cheek,
But not take in the mind.
CAM.   Yea, say you so ?
There shall not at your father's house these seven years   570
Be born another such.
FLO.   My good Camillo,
She is as forward of her breeding as
She is i' th' rear o' our birth.
CAM.   I cannot say 'tis pity
She lacks instructions, for she seems a mistress
To most that teach.
PER.   Your pardon, sir ; for this   575
I'll blush you thanks.
FLO.   My prettiest Perdita !
But, O, the thorns we stand upon !   Camillo—
Preserver of my father, now of me ;
The medicine of our house—how shall we do ?
We are not furnish'd like Bohemia's son ;   580
Nor shall appear in Sicilia.
CAM.   My lord,
Fear none of this.   I think you know my fortunes
Do all lie there.   It shall be so my care
To have you royally appointed as if
The scene you play were mine.   For instance, sir,   585

That you may know you shall not want—one word.

[they talk aside.

Re-enter AUTOLYCUS.

AUT. Ha, ha ! what a fool Honesty is ! and Trust, his sworn brother,
a very simple gentleman ! I have sold all my trumpery ; not a
counterfeit stone, not a ribbon, glass, pomander, brooch, table-
book, ballad, knife, tape, glove, shoe-tie, bracelet, horn-ring, to
keep my pack from fasting. They throng who should buy first,
as if my trinkets had been hallowed and brought a benediction
to the buyer ; by which means I saw whose purse was best in
picture ; and what I saw, to my good use I rememb'red. My
clown, who wants but something to be a reasonable man, grew so
in love with the wenches' song that he would not stir his pettitoes
till he had both tune and words, which so drew the rest of the herd
to me that all their other senses stuck in ears. You might have
pinch'd a placket, it was senseless ; 'twas nothing to geld a cod-
piece of a purse ; I would have fil'd keys off that hung in chains.
No hearing, no feeling, but my sir's song, and admiring the
nothing of it. So that in this time of lethargy I pick'd and cut
most of their festival purses ; and had not the old man come in
with a whoobub against his daughter and the King's son and
scar'd my choughs from the chaff, I had not left a purse alive in
the whole army. [CAMILLO, FLORIZEL, *and* PERDITA, *come forward.*

CAM. Nay, but my letters, by this means being there   610
So soon as you arrive, shall clear that doubt.

FLO. And those that you'll procure from King Leontes ?

CAM.   Shall satisfy your father.

PER.   Happy be you !

All that you speak shows fair.

CAM. [*seeing* AUTOLYCUS.] Who have we here ?
We'll make an instrument of this ; omit   615
Nothing may give us aid.

AUT. [*aside.*] If they have overheard me now—why, hanging.

CAM. How now, good fellow ! Why shak'st thou so ? Fear not,
man ; here's no harm intended to thee.

AUT. I am a poor fellow, sir.   620

CAM. Why, be so still ; here's nobody will steal that from thee.
Yet for the outside of thy poverty we must make an exchange ;
therefore discase thee instantly—thou must think there's a
necessity in't—and change garments with this gentleman.
Though the pennyworth on his side be the worst, yet hold thee,
there's some boot.   [*giving money.*

AUT. I am a poor fellow, sir. [*aside.*] I know ye well enough.

CAM. Nay, prithee dispatch. The gentleman is half flay'd already.

AUT. Are you in earnest, sir ? [*aside.*] I smell the trick on't.

FLO. Dispatch, I prithee.

AUT. Indeed, I have had earnest ; but I cannot with conscience
take it.   636

CAM. Unbuckle, unbuckle. [FLORIZEL *and* AUTOLYCUS *exchange gar-*
ments.

Fortunate mistress—let my prophecy
Come home to ye !—you must retire yourself
Into some covert ; take your sweetheart's hat   640

And pluck it o'er your brows, muffle your face,
Dismantle you, and, as you can, disliken
The truth of your own seeming, that you may—
For I do fear eyes over—to shipboard
Get undescried.
PER.   I see the play so lies   645
That I must bear a part.
CAM.   No remedy.
Have you done there?
FLO.   Should I now meet my father,
He would not call me son.
CAM.   Nay, you shall have no hat.
                              [*giving it to* PERDITA.
Come, lady, come.   Farewell, my friend.   Line 649, 'Come,
AUT.   Adieu, sir.   lady . . . Adieu, sir', is
FLO. O Perdita, what have we twain forgot!   650   spoken after line 657.
Pray you a word.   [*they converse apart.*
CAM. [*aside.*]   What I do next shall be to tell the King
Of this escape, and whither they are bound;
Wherein my hope is I shall so prevail
To force him after; in whose company   655
I shall re-view Sicilia, for whose sight
I have a woman's longing.   Line 649 spoken
FLO.   Fortune speed us!   here.
Thus we set on, Camillo, to th' sea-side.
CAM. The swifter speed the better.   659
                    [*exeunt* FLORIZEL, PERDITA, *and* CAMILLO.
AUT. I understand the business, I hear it.   To have an open ear,
a quick eye, and a nimble hand, is necessary for a cut-purse;
a good nose is requisite also, to smell out work for th' other senses.
I see this is the time that the unjust man doth thrive.   What an
exchange has this been without boot!   What a boot is here with
this exchange!   Sure, the gods do this year connive at us, and
we may do anything extempore.   The Prince himself is about a
piece of iniquity—stealing away from his father with his clog at
his heels.   If I thought it were a piece of honesty to acquaint the
King withal, I would not do't.   I hold it the more knavery to
conceal it; and therein am I constant to my profession.   672

Re-enter CLOWN *and* SHEI HERD.

Aside, aside—here is more matter for a hot brain.   Every lane's
end, every shop, church, session, hanging, yields a careful man
work.   675
CLO. See, see; what a man you are now!   There is no other way
but to tell the King she's a changeling and none of your flesh
and blood.
SHEP. Nay, but hear me.
CLO. Nay—but hear me.   680
SHEP. Go to, then.
CLO. She being none of your flesh and blood, your flesh and blood
has not offended the King; and so your flesh and blood is not to
be punish'd by him.   Show those things you found about her,
those secret things—all but what she has with her.   This being
done, let the law go whistle; I warrant you.   687

SHEP. I will tell the King all, every word—yea, and his son's pranks too ; who, I may say, is no honest man, neither to his father nor to me, to go about to make me the King's brother-in-law.   691

CLO. Indeed, brother-in-law was the farthest off you could have been to him ; and then your blood had been the dearer by I know how much an ounce.

AUT. [aside.]   Very wisely, puppies !

SHEP. Well, let us to the King.   There is that in this fardel will make him scratch his beard.

AUT. [aside.]   I know not what impediment this complaint may be to the flight of my master.

CLO. Pray heartily he be at palace.   700

AUT. [aside.]   Though I am not naturally honest, I am so sometimes by chance.   Let me pocket up my pedlar's excrement. [takes off his false beard.]   How now, rustics !   Whither are you bound ?

SHEP. To th' palace, an it like your worship.

AUT. Your affairs there, what, with whom, the condition of that fardel, the place of your dwelling, your names, your ages, of what having, breeding, and anything that is fitting to be known—discover.

CLO. We are but plain fellows, sir.   710

AUT. A lie : you are rough and hairy.   Let me have no lying ; it becomes none but tradesmen, and they often give us soldiers the lie ; but we pay them for it with stamped coin, not stabbing steel ; therefore they do not give us the lie.   715

CLO. Your worship had like to have given us one, if you had not taken yourself with the manner.

SHEP. Are you a courtier, an't like you, sir ?

AUT. Whether it like me or no, I am a courtier.   Seest thou not the air of the court in these enfoldings ?   Hath not my gait in it the measure of the court ?   Receives not thy nose court-odour from me ?   Reflect I not on thy baseness court-contempt ?   Think'st thou, for that I insinuate, that toaze from thee thy business, I am therefore no courtier ?   I am courtier cap-a-pe, and one that will either push on or pluck back thy business there ; whereupon I command thee to open thy affair.   727

SHEP. My business, sir, is to the King.

AUT. What advocate hast thou to him ?

SHEP. I know not, an't like you.

CLO. Advocate's the court-word for a pheasant ; say you have none.

SHEP. None, sir ; I have no pheasant, cock or hen.

AUT. How blessed are we that are not simple men !
      Yet nature might have made me as these are,   735
      Therefore I will not disdain.

CLO. This cannot be but a great courtier.

SHEP. His garments are rich, but he wears them not handsomely.

CLO. He seems to be the more noble in being fantastical.   A great man, I'll warrant ; I know by the picking on's teeth.   742

AUT. The fardel there ?   What's i' th' fardel ?   Wherefore that box ?

SHEP. Sir, there lies such secrets in this fardel and box which none must know but the King ; and which he shall know within this hour, if I may come to th' speech of him.

AUT. Age, thou hast lost thy labour.

SHEP. Why, sir ?   750

AUT. The King is not at the palace ; he is gone aboard a new ship to

'and they often . . . with the manner' omitted.

purge melancholy and air himself ; for, if thou be'st capable of things serious, thou must know the King is full of grief.

SHEP. So 'tis said, sir—about his son, that should have married a shepherd's daughter.

AUT. If that shepherd be not in hand-fast, let him fly ; the curses he shall have, the tortures he shall feel, will break the back of man, the heart of monster.

CLO. Think you so, sir ?   760

AUT. Not he alone shall suffer what wit can make heavy and vengeance bitter ; but those that are germane to him, though remov'd fifty times, shall all come under the hangman—which, though it be great pity! yet it is necessary. An old sheep-whistling rogue, a ram-tender, to offer to have his daughter come into grace ! Some say he shall be ston'd ; but that death is too soft for him, say I. Draw our throne into a sheep-cote !—all deaths are too few, the sharpest too easy.   770

CLO. Has the old man e'er a son, sir, do you hear, an't like you, sir ?

AUT. He has a son—who shall be flay'd alive ; then 'nointed over with honey, set on the head of a wasp's nest ; then stand till he be three quarters and a dram dead ; then recover'd again with aqua-vitæ or some other hot infusion ; then, raw as he is, and in the hottest day prognostication proclaims, shall he be set against a brick wall, the sun looking with a southward eye upon him, where he is to behold him with flies blown to death. But what talk we of these traitorly rascals, whose miseries are to be smil'd at, their offences being so capital ? Tell me, for you seem to be honest plain men, what you have to the King. Being something gently consider'd, I'll bring you where he is aboard, tender your persons to his presence, whisper him in your behalfs ; and if it be in man besides the King to effect your suits, here is man shall do it.   788

CLO. He seems to be of great authority. Close with him, give him gold ; and though authority be a stubborn bear, yet he is oft led by the nose with gold. Show the inside of your purse to the outside of his hand, and no more ado. Remember—ston'd and flay'd alive.

SHEP. An't please you, sir, to undertake the business for us, here is that gold I have. I'll make it as much more, and leave this young man in pawn till I bring it you.   797

AUT. After I have done what I promised ?

SHEP. Ay, sir.

AUT. Well, give me the moiety. Are you a party in this business ?

CLO. In some sort, sir ; but though my case be a pitiful one, I hope I shall not be flay'd out of it.

AUT. O, that's the case of the shepherd's son ! Hang him, he'll be made an example.   805

CLO. Comfort, good comfort ! We must to the King and show our strange sights. He must know 'tis none of your daughter nor my sister ; we are gone else. Sir, I will give you as much as this old man does, when the business is performed ; and remain, as he says, your pawn till it be brought you.   811

AUT. I will trust you. Walk before toward the sea-side ; go on the right-hand ; I will but look upon the hedge, and follow you.

CLO. We are blest in this man, as I may say, even blest.   815

SHEP. Let's before, as he bids us.   He was provided to do us good.
                              [*exeunt* SHEPHERD *and* CLOWN.
AUT. If I had a mind to be honest, I see Fortune would not suffer me :
she drops booties in my mouth.   I am courted now with a double
occasion—gold, and a means to do the Prince my master good ;
which who knows how that may turn back to my advancement ?
I will bring these two moles, these blind ones, aboard him.   If he
think it fit to shore them again, and that the complaint they have
to the King concerns him nothing, let him call me rogue for being
so far officious ; for I am proof against that title, and what shame
else belongs to't.   To him will I present them.   There may be
matter in it.   [*exit.*

ACT FIVE.

SCENE I.   *Sicilia.*   *The palace of* LEONTES.

Enter LEONTES, CLEOMENES, DION, PAULINA, *and* OTHERS.

SCENE 13
Interior. Sicily.
Palace. Day.

CLEO. Sir, you have done enough, and have perform'd
A saint-like sorrow.   No fault could you make
Which you have not redeem'd ; indeed, paid down
More penitence than done trespass.   At the last,
Do as the heavens have done : forget your evil ;   5
With them forgive yourself.
LEON.   Whilst I remember
Her and her virtues, I cannot forget
My blemishes in them, and so still think of
The wrong I did myself ; which was so much
That heirless it hath made my kingdom, and   10
Destroy'd the sweet'st companion that e'er man
Bred his hopes out of.
PAUL.   True, too true, my lord.
If, one by one, you wedded all the world
Or from the all that are took something good
To make a perfect woman, she you kill'd   15
Would be unparallel'd.
LEON.   I think so.   Kill'd !
She I kill'd !   I did so ; but thou strik'st me
Sorely, to say I did.   It is as bitter
Upon thy tongue as in my thought.   Now, good now,
Say so but seldom.
CLEO.   Not at all, good lady.   20
You might have spoken a thousand things that would
Have done the time more benefit, and grac'd
Your kindness better.
PAUL.   You are one of those
Would have him wed again.
DION.   If you would not so,
You pity not the state, nor the remembrance   25
Of his most sovereign name ; consider little
What dangers, by his Highness' fail of issue,
May drop upon his kingdom and devour
Incertain lookers-on.   What were more holy
Than to rejoice the former queen is well ?   30
What holier than, for royalty's repair,

For present comfort, and for future good,
To bless the bed of majesty again
With a sweet fellow to't?
PAUL.   There is none worthy,
Respecting her that's gone. Besides, the gods   35
Will have fulfill'd their secret purposes ;
For has not the divine Apollo said,
Is't not the tenour of his oracle,
That King Leontes shall not have an heir
Till his lost child be found ? Which that it shall,   40
Is all as monstrous to our human reason
As my Antigonus to break his grave
And come again to me ; who, on my life,
Did perish with the infant. 'Tis your counsel
My lord should to the heavens be contrary,   45
Oppose against their wills. [to LEONTES.] Care not for issue ;
The crown will find an heir. Great Alexander
Left his to th' worthiest ; so his successor
Was like to be the best.
LEON.   Good Paulina,
Who hast the memory of Hermione,   50
I know, in honour, O that ever I
Had squar'd me to thy counsel ! Then, even now,
I might have look'd upon my queen's full eyes,
Have taken treasure from her lips—
PAUL.   And left them
More rich for what they yielded.
LEON.   Thou speak'st truth.   55
No more such wives ; therefore, no wife. One worse,
And better us'd, would make her sainted spirit
Again possess her corpse, and on this stage,
Where we offend her now, appear soul-vex'd,
And begin ' Why to me '—
PAUL.   Had she such power,   60
She had just cause.
LEON. She had ; and would incense me
To murder her I married.
PAUL.   I should so.
Were I the ghost that walk'd, I'd bid you mark
Her eye, and tell me for what dull part in't
You chose her ; then I'd shriek, that even your ears   65
Should rift to hear me ; and the words that follow'd
Should be ' Remember mine '.
LEON.   Stars, stars,
And all eyes else dead coals ! Fear thou no wife ;
I'll have no wife, Paulina.
PAUL.   Will you swear
Never to marry but by my free leave ?   70
LEON. Never, Paulina ; so be blest my spirit !
PAUL. Then, good my lords, bear witness to his oath.
CLEO. You tempt him over-much.
PAUL.   Unless another,
As like Hermione as is her picture,
Affront his eye.

Line 59: for 'Where
we offend her now'
read 'Were we
offenders now'.

88

CLEO.   Good madam—
PAUL.   I have done.   75
Yet, if my lord will marry—if you will, sir,
No remedy but you will—give me the office
To choose you a queen.   She shall not be so young
As was your former ; but she shall be such
As, walk'd your first queen's ghost, it should take joy   80
To see her in your arms.
LEON.   My true Paulina,
We shall not marry till thou bid'st us.
PAUL.   That
Shall be when your first queen's again in breath ;
Never till then.

                    Enter a GENTLEMAN.   GENTLEMAN is played
                                                                     by LEONTES'
GENT. One that gives out himself Prince Florizel,   85   SERVANT.
Son of Polixenes, with his princess—she
The fairest I have yet beheld—desires access
To your high presence.
LEON. What with him ?   He comes not
Like to his father's greatness.   His approach,
So out of circumstance and sudden, tells us   90
'Tis not a visitation fram'd, but forc'd
By need and accident.   What train ?
GENT.   But few,
And those but mean.
LEON. His princess, say you, with him ?
GENT. Ay ; the most peerless piece of earth, I think,
That e'er the sun shone bright on.
PAUL.   O Hermione,   95
As every present time doth boast itself
Above a better gone, so must thy grave
Give way to what's seen now !   Sir, you yourself
Have said and writ so, but your writing now
Is colder than that theme : ' She had not been,   100
Nor was not to be equall'd '.   Thus your verse
Flow'd with her beauty once ; 'tis shrewdly ebb'd,
To say you have seen a better.
GENT.   Pardon, madam.
The one I have almost forgot—your pardon ;
The other, when she has obtain'd your eye,   105
Will have your tongue too.   This is a creature,
Would she begin a sect, might quench the zeal
Of all professors else, make proselytes
Of who she but bid follow.
PAUL.   How ! not women ?
GENT. Women will love her that she is a woman   110
More worth than any man ; men, that she is
The rarest of all women.
LEON.   Go, Cleomenes ;
Yourself, assisted with your honour'd friends,
Bring them to our embracement.   [*exeunt.*
                              Still, 'tis strange
He thus should steal upon us.

Perdita (Debbie Farrington) and Florizel (Robin Kermode) are presented to Leontes (Jeremy Kemp) by Paulina (Margaret Tyzack)

PAUL.   Had our prince,   115
  Jewel of children, seen this hour, he had pair'd
  Well with this lord ; there was not full a month
  Between their births.
LEON. Prithee no more ; cease. Thou know'st
  He dies to me again when talk'd of. Sure,   120
  When I shall see this gentleman, thy speeches
  Will bring me to consider that which may
  Unfurnish me of reason.

    Re-enter CLEOMENES, *with* FLORIZEL, PERDITA, *and* ATTENDANTS.

              They are come.
  Your mother was most true to wedlock, Prince ;
  For she did print your royal father off,   125
  Conceiving you. Were I but twenty-one,
  Your father's image is so hit in you,
  His very air, that I should call you brother,
  As I did him, and speak of something wildly
  By us perform'd before. Most dearly welcome !   130
  And your fair princess—goddess ! O, alas !
  I lost a couple that 'twixt heaven and earth
  Might thus have stood begetting wonder as
  You, gracious couple, do. And then I lost—
  All mine own folly—the society,   135
  Amity too, of your brave father, whom,
  Though bearing misery, I desire my life
  Once more to look on him.
FLO.   By his command
  Have I here touch'd Sicilia, and from him
  Give you all greetings that a king, at friend,   140
  Can send his brother ; and, but infirmity,
  Which waits upon worn times, hath something seiz'd
  His wish'd ability, he had himself
  The lands and waters 'twixt your throne and his
  Measur'd, to look upon you ; whom he loves,   145
  He bade me say so, more than all the sceptres
  And those that bear them living.
LEON.   O my brother—
  Good gentleman !—the wrongs I have done thee stir
  Afresh within me ; and these thy offices,
  So rarely kind, are as interpreters   150
  Of my behind-hand slackness ! Welcome hither,
  As is the spring to th' earth. And hath he too
  Expos'd this paragon to th' fearful usage,
  At least ungentle, of the dreadful Neptune,
  To greet a man not worth her pains, much less   155
  Th' adventure of her person ?
FLO.   Good, my lord,
  She came from Libya.
LEON.   Where the warlike Smalus,
  That noble honour'd lord, is fear'd and lov'd ?
FLO. Most royal sir, from thence ; from him whose daughter
  His tears proclaim'd his, parting with her ; thence,   160
  A prosperous south-wind friendly, we have cross'd,

To execute the charge my father gave me
For visiting your Highness. My best train
I have from your Sicilian shores dismiss'd ;
Who for Bohemia bend, to signify   165
Not only my success in Libya, sir,
But my arrival and my wife's in safety
Here where we are.
LEON.   The blessed gods
Purge all infection from our air whilst you
Do climate here ! You have a holy father,   170
A graceful gentleman, against whose person,
So sacred as it is, I have done sin,
For which the heavens, taking angry note,
Have left me issueless ; and your father's blest,
As he from heaven merits it, with you,   175
Worthy his goodness. What might I have been,
Might I a son and daughter now have look'd on,
Such goodly things as you !

Enter a LORD.   *Enter* I LORD.

LORD.   Most noble sir,
That which I shall report will bear no credit,
Were not the proof so nigh. Please you, great sir,   180
Bohemia greets you from himself by me ;
Desires you to attach his son, who has—
His dignity and duty both cast off—
Fled from his father, from his hopes, and with
A shepherd's daughter.
LEON.   Where's Bohemia ? Speak.   185
LORD. Here in your city ; I now came from him.
I speak amazedly ; and it becomes
My marvel and my message. To your court
Whiles he was hast'ning—in the chase, it seems,
Of this fair couple—meets he on the way   190
The father of this seeming lady and
Her brother, having both their country quitted
With this young prince.
FLO.   Camillo has betray'd me ;
Whose honour and whose honesty till now
Endur'd all weathers.
LORD.   Lay't so to his charge ;   195
He's with the King your father.
LEON.   Who ? Camillo ?
LORD. Camillo, sir ; I spake with him ; who now
Has these poor men in question. Never saw I
Wretches so quake. They kneel, they kiss the earth ;
Forswear themselves as often as they speak.   200
Bohemia stops his ears, and threatens them
With divers deaths in death.
PER.   O my poor father !
The heaven sets spies upon us, will not have
Our contract celebrated.
LEON.   You are married ?
FLO We are not, sir, nor are we like to be ;   205

The stars, I see, will kiss the valleys first.
The odds for high and low's alike.
LEON.   My lord,
Is this the daughter of a king ?
FLO.   She is,
When once she is my wife.
LEON. That ' once ', I see by your good father's speed,   210
Will come on very slowly.   I am sorry,
Most sorry, you have broken from his liking
Where you were tied in duty ; and as sorry
Your choice is not so rich in worth as beauty,
That you might well enjoy her.
FLO.   Dear, look up.   215
Though Fortune, visible an enemy,
Should chase us with my father, pow'r no jot
Hath she to change our loves.   Beseech you, sir,
Remember since you ow'd no more to time
Than I do now.   With thought of such affections,   220
Step forth mine advocate ; at your request
My father will grant precious things as trifles.
LEON.   Would he do so, I'd beg your precious mistress,
Which he counts but a trifle.
PAUL.   Sir, my liege,
Your eye hath too much youth in't.   Not a month   225
Fore your queen died, she was more worth such gazes
Than what you look on now.
LEON.   I thought of her
Even in these looks I made. [to FLORIZEL.]   But your petition
Is yet unanswer'd.   I will to your father.
Your honour not o'erthrown by your desires,   230
I am friend to them and you.   Upon which errand
I now go toward him ; therefore, follow me,
And mark what way I make.   Come, good my lord.   [exeunt.

SCENE II.   *Sicilia.   Before the palace of Leontes.*

Enter AUTOLYCUS *and a* GENTLEMAN.

AUT. Beseech you, sir, were you present at this relation ?
1 GENT. I was by at the opening of the fardel, heard the old shepherd
    deliver the manner how he found it ; whereupon, after a little
    amazedness, we were all commanded out of the chamber ; only
    this, methought I heard the shepherd say he found the child.   7
AUT. I would most gladly know the issue of it.
1 GENT. I make a broken delivery of the business ; but the changes I
    perceived in the King and Camillo were very notes of admiration.
    They seem'd almost, with staring on one another, to tear the
    cases of their eyes ; there was speech in their dumbness, language
    in their very gesture ; they look'd as they had heard of a world
    ransom'd, or one destroyed. A notable passion of wonder
    appeared in them ; but the wisest beholder that knew no more
    but seeing could not say if th' importance were joy or sorrow—
    but in the extremity of the one it must needs be.   19

Enter another GENTLEMAN.

SCENE 14
*Exterior. Sicily.
Palace Garden. Day.*
Other Lords and
townspeople are in
the background.
1 GENTLEMAN is
played by 2 LORD.

2 GENTLEMAN is
played by 1 LORD.

Here comes a gentleman that happily knows more. The news,
Rogero ?

2 GENT. Nothing but bonfires. The oracle is fulfill'd : the King's
daughter is found. Such a deal of wonder is broken out within
this hour that ballad-makers cannot be able to express it. 25

Enter another GENTLEMAN.

Here comes the Lady Paulina's steward ; he can deliver you more.
How goes it now, sir ? This news, which is call'd true, is so like
an old tale that the verity of it is in strong suspicion. Has the
King found his heir ? 29

3 GENT. Most true, if ever truth were pregnant by circumstance.
That which you hear you'll swear you see, there is such unity
in the proofs. The mantle of Queen Hermione's ; her jewel
about the neck of it ; the letters of Antigonus found with it,
which they know to be his character ; the majesty of the creature
in resemblance of the mother ; the affection of nobleness which
nature shows above her breeding ; and many other evidences—
proclaim her with all certainty to be the King's daughter. Did
you see the meeting of the two kings ?

2 GENT. No. 40

3 GENT. Then you have lost a sight which was to be seen, cannot be
spoken of. There might you have beheld one joy crown another,
so and in such manner that it seem'd sorrow wept to take leave
of them ; for their joy waded in tears. There was casting up of
eyes, holding up of hands, with countenance of such distraction
that they were to be known by garment, not by favour. Our
king, being ready to leap out of himself for joy of his found
daughter, as if that joy were now become a loss, cries ' O, thy
mother, thy mother ! ' then asks Bohemia forgiveness ; then
embraces his son-in-law ; then again worries he his daughter
with clipping her. Now he thanks the old shepherd, which
stands by like a weather-bitten conduit of many king's reigns.
I never heard of such another encounter, which lames report to
follow it and undoes description to do it. 56

2 GENT. What, pray you, became of Antigonus, that carried hence the
child ?

3 GENT. Like an old tale still, which will have matter to rehearse,
though credit be asleep and not an ear open : he was torn to
pieces with a bear. This avouches the shepherd's son, who has
not only his innocence, which seems much, to justify him, but a
handkerchief and rings of his that Paulina knows.

I GENT. What became of his bark and his followers ? 66

3 GENT. Wreck'd the same instant of their master's death, and in
the view of the shepherd ; so that all the instruments which
aided to expose the child were even then lost when it was found.
But, O, the noble combat that 'twixt joy and sorrow was fought
in Paulina ! She had one eye declin'd for the loss of her husband,
another elevated that the oracle was fulfill'd. She lifted the
Princess from the earth, and so locks her in embracing as if she
would pin her to her heart, that she might no more be in danger
of losing. 76

I GENT. The dignity of this act was worth the audience of kings and
princes ; for by such was it acted.

3 GENT. One of the prettiest touches of all, and that which angl'd for

3 GENTLEMAN is
played by PAULINA'S
STEWARD.

Spoken by all the
Lords.

mine eyes—caught the water, though not the fish—was, when at
the relation of the Queen's death, with the manner how she came
to't bravely confess'd and lamented by the King, how attentiveness
wounded his daughter ; till, from one sign of dolour to another, she
did with an ' Alas ! '—I would fain say—bleed tears ; for I am
sure my heart wept blood.   Who was most marble there changed
colour ; some swooned, all sorrowed.   If all the world could have
seen't, the woe had been universal.

1 GENT. Are they returned to the court ?   90

3 GENT. No.   The Princess hearing of her mother's statue, which is
in the keeping of Paulina—a piece many years in doing and now
newly perform'd by that rare Italian master, Julio Romano, who,
had he himself eternity and could put breath into his work, would
beguile nature of her custom, so perfectly he is her ape.   He so
near to Hermione hath done Hermione that they say one would
speak to her and stand in hope of answer—thither with all
greediness of affection are they gone, and there they intend to sup.

2 GENT. I thought she had some great matter there in hand ; for she
hath privately twice or thrice a day, ever since the death of Hermione, visited that removed house.   Shall we thither, and with
our company piece the rejoicing ?   105

1 GENT. Who would be thence that has the benefit of access ?   Every
wink of an eye some new grace will be born.   Our absence makes
us unthrifty to our knowledge.   Let's along.   [*exeunt* GENTLEMEN.

AUT. Now, had I not the dash of my former life in me, would preferment drop on my head.   I brought the old man and his son aboard
the Prince ; told him I heard them talk of a fardel and I know not
what ; but he at that time over-fond of the shepherd's daughter—
so he then took her to be—who began to be much sea-sick, and
himself little better, extremity of weather continuing, this mystery
remained undiscover'd.   But 'tis all one to me ; for had I been
the finder-out of this secret, it would not have relish'd among my
other discredits.   119

Enter SHEPHERD *and* CLOWN.

Here come those I have done good to against my will, and already
appearing in the blossoms of their fortune.

SHEP. Come, boy ; I am past moe children, but thy sons and daughters
will be all gentlemen born.   123

CLO. You are well met, sir.   You denied to fight with me this other
day, because I was no gentleman born.   See you these clothes ?
Say you see them not and think me still no gentleman born.
You were best say these robes are not gentlemen born.   Give me
the lie, do ; and try whether I am not now a gentleman born.

AUT. I know you are now, sir, a gentleman born.   130

CLO. Ay, and have been so any time these four hours.

SHEP. And so have I, boy.

CLO. So you have ; but I was a gentleman born before my father ;
for the King's son took me by the hand and call'd me brother ;
and then the two kings call'd my father brother ; and then the
Prince, my brother, and the Princess, my sister, call'd my father
father.   And so we wept ; and there was the first gentleman-like
tears that ever we shed.

SHEP. We may live, son, to shed many more.   140

CLO. Ay ; or else 'twere hard luck, being in so preposterous estate
as we are.

AUT. I humbly beseech you, sir, to pardon me all the faults I have
committed to your worship, and to give me your good report to
the Prince my master.   145

SHEP. Prithee, son, do ; for we must be gentle, now we are gentlemen.

CLO. Thou wilt amend thy life ?

AUT. Ay, an it like your good worship.

CLO. Give me thy hand.   I will swear to the Prince thou art as honest
a true fellow as any is in Bohemia.   151

SHEP. You may say it, but not swear it.

CLO. Not swear it, now I am a gentleman ?   Let boors and franklins
say it :   I'll swear it.

SHEP. How if it be false, son ?   155

CLO. If it be ne'er so false, a true gentleman may swear it in the
behalf of his friend.   And I'll swear to the Prince thou art a tall
fellow of thy hands and that thou wilt not be drunk ; but I know
thou art no tall fellow of thy hands and that thou wilt be drunk.
But I'll swear it ; and I would thou wouldst be a tall fellow of thy
hands.   161

AUT. I will prove so, sir, to my power.

CLO. Ay, by any means, prove a tall fellow.   If I do not wonder how
thou dar'st venture to be drunk not being a tall fellow, trust me
not.   Hark ! the kings and the princes, our kindred, are going
to see the Queen's picture.   Come, follow us ; we'll be thy good
masters.   [*exeunt.*

SCENE III.   *Sicilia.   A chapel in* PAULINA'S *house.*

Enter LEONTES, POLIXENES, FLORIZEL, PERDITA, CAMILLO, PAULINA,
LORDS *and* ATTENDANTS.

LEON. O grave and good Paulina, the great comfort
That I have had of thee !

PAUL.   What, sovereign sir,
I did not well, I meant well.   All my services
You have paid home ; but that you have vouchsaf'd,
With your crown'd brother and these your contracted   5
Heirs of your kingdoms, my poor house to visit,
It is a surplus of your grace, which never
My life may last to answer.

LEON.   O Paulina,
We honour you with trouble ; but we came
To see the statue of our queen.   Your gallery   10
Have we pass'd through, not without much content
In many singularities ; but we saw not
That which my daughter came to look upon,
The statue of her mother.

PAUL.   As she liv'd peerless.
So her dead likeness, I do well believe,   15
Excels whatever yet you look'd upon
Or hand of man hath done ; therefore I keep it
Lonely, apart.   But here it is.   Prepare
To see the life as lively mock'd as ever
Still sleep mock'd death.   Behold ; and say 'tis well.   20

[PAULINA *draws a curtain, and discovers* HERMIONE *standing like a statue.*

SCENE 15
*Interior. Sicily.
Paulina's House.
Day.*

I like your silence ; it the more shows off
Your wonder ; but yet speak. First, you, my liege.
Comes it not something near ?
LEON.   Her natural posture !‾
Chide me, dear stone, that I may say indeed
Thou art Hermione ; or rather, thou art she   25
In thy not chiding ; for she was as tender
As infancy and grace. But yet, Paulina,
Hermione was not so much wrinkled, nothing
So aged as this seems.
POL.   O, not by much !
PAUL. So much the more our carver's excellence,   30
Which lets go by some sixteen years and makes her
As she liv'd now.
LEON.   As now she might have done,
So much to my good comfort as it is
Now piercing to my soul. O, thus she stood,
Even with such life of majesty—warm life,   35
As now it coldly stands—when first I woo'd her !
I am asham'd. Does not the stone rebuke me
For being more stone than it ? O royal piece,
There's magic in thy majesty, which has
My evils conjur'd to remembrance, and   40
From thy admiring daughter took the spirits,
Standing like stone with thee !
PER.   And give me leave,
And do not say 'tis superstition that
I kneel, and then implore her blessing. Lady,
Dear queen, that ended when I but began,   45
Give me that hand of yours to kiss.
PAUL.   O, patience !
The statue is but newly fix'd, the colour's
Not dry.
CAM. My lord, your sorrow was too sore laid on,
Which sixteen winters cannot blow away,   50
So many summers dry. Scarce any joy
Did ever so long live ; no sorrow
But kill'd itself much sooner.
POL.   Dear my brother,
Let him that was the cause of this have pow'r
To take off so much grief from you as he   55
Will piece up in himself.
PAUL.   Indeed, my lord,
If I had thought the sight of my poor image
Would thus have wrought you—for the stone is mine—
I'd not have show'd it.
LEON.   Do not draw the curtain.
PAUL. No longer shall you gaze on't, lest your fancy   60
May think anon it moves.
LEON.   Let be, let be.
Would I were dead, but that methinks already—
What was he that did make it ? See, my lord,
Would you not deem it breath'd, and that those veins
Did verily bear blood ?

POL.   Masterly done!   65
  The very life seems warm upon her lip.
LEON. The fixture of her eye has motion in't,
  As we are mock'd with art.
PAUL.   I'll draw the curtain.
  My lord's almost so far transported that
  He'll think anon it lives.
LEON.   O sweet Paulina,   70
  Make me to think so twenty years together!
  No settled senses of the world can match
  The pleasure of that madness.   Let't alone.
PAUL. I am sorry, sir, I have thus far stirr'd you ; but
  I could afflict you farther.
LEON.   Do, Paulina ;   75
  For this affliction has a taste as sweet
  As any cordial comfort.   Still, methinks,
  There is an air comes from her.   What fine chisel
  Could ever yet cut breath ?   Let no man mock me,
  For I will kiss her.
PAUL.   Good my lord, forbear.   80
  The ruddiness upon her lip is wet ;
  You'll mar it if you kiss it ; stain your own
  With oily painting.   Shall I draw the curtain ?
LEON. No, not these twenty years.
FER.   So long could I
  Stand by, a looker-on.
PAUL.   Either forbear,   85
  Quit presently the chapel, or resolve you
  For more amazement.   If you can behold it,
  I'll make the statue move indeed, descend,
  And take you by the hand, but then you'll think—
  Which I protest against—I am assisted   90
  By wicked powers.
LEON.   What you can make her do
  I am content to look on ; what to speak
  I am content to hear ; for 'tis as easy
  To make her speak as move.
PAUL.   It is requir'd
  You do awake your faith.   Then all stand still ;   95
  Or those that think it is unlawful business
  I am about, let them depart.
LEON.   Proceed.
  No foot shall stir.
PAUL. Music, awake her : strike.   [music.
  'Tis time ; descend ; be stone no more ; approach ;
  Strike all that look upon with marvel.   Come ;   100
  I'll fill your grave up.   Stir ; nay, come away.
  Bequeath to death your numbness, for from him
  Dear life redeems you.   You perceive she stirs.
                   [HERMIONE comes down from the pedestal.
  Start not ; her actions shall be holy as
  You hear my spell is lawful.   Do not shun her   105
  Until you see her die again ; for then
  You kill her double.   Nay, present your hand.

When she was young you woo'd her ; now in age
Is she become the suitor ?
LEON.   O, she's warm !   110
If this be magic, let it be an art
Lawful as eating.
POL.   She embraces him.
CAM. She hangs about his neck.
If she pertain to life, let her speak too.
POL. Ay, and make it manifest where she has liv'd,
Or how stol'n from the dead.
PAUL.   That she is living,   115
Were it but told you, should be hooted at
Like an old tale ; but it appears she lives
Though yet she speak not. Mark a little while.
Please you to interpose, fair madam. Kneel,
And pray your mother's blessing. Turn, good lady ;   120
Our Perdita is found.
HER.   You gods, look down,
And from your sacred vials pour your graces
Upon my daughter's head ! Tell me, mine own,
Where hast thou been preserv'd ? Where liv'd ? How found
Thy father's court ? For thou shalt hear that I,   125
Knowing by Paulina that the oracle
Gave hope thou wast in being, have preserv'd
Myself to see the issue.
PAUL.   There's time enough for that,
Lest they desire upon this push to trouble
Your joys with like relation. Go together,   130
You precious winners all ; your exultation
Partake to every one. I, an old turtle,
Will wing me to some wither'd bough, and there
My mate, that's never to be found again,
Lament till I am lost.
LEON.   O peace, Paulina !   135
Thou shouldst a husband take by my consent,
As I by thine a wife. This is a match,
And made between's by vows. Thou hast found mine ;
But how, is to be question'd ; for I saw her,
As I thought, dead ; and have, in vain, said many   140
A prayer upon her grave. I'll not seek far—
For him, I partly know his mind—to find thee
An honourable husband. Come, Camillo,
And take her by the hand whose worth and honesty
Is richly noted, and here justified   145
By us, a pair of kings. Let's from this place.
What ! look upon my brother. Both your pardons,
That e'er I put between your holy looks
My ill suspicion. This your son-in-law,
And son unto the King, whom heavens directing,   150
Is troth-plight to your daughter. Good Paulina,
Lead us from hence where we may leisurely
Each one demand and answer to his part
Perform'd in this wide gap of time since first
We were dissever'd. Hastily lead away.   [exeunt.

99

GLOSSARY

Difficult phrases are listed under the most important or most difficult words in them. If no such word stands out, they are listed under the first word.

Words appear in the form they take in the text. If they occur in several forms, they are listed under the root form (singular for nouns, infinitive for verbs).

Line references are given only when the same word is used with different meanings, and when there are puns.

Line numbers of prose passages are counted from the last numbered line before the line referred to (since the numbers given do not always correspond to those in this edition).

ABIDE, stay briefly
ABILITY, *see* SEIZ'D, V i 143
ABOARD HIM, to him aboard his ship
ABOUT, i.e. near, II i 59, II iii 43
ABROAD, at large, IV iv 248
ABUS'D, deceived
ACCOUNT (n.), 'beyond account', beyond record, unprecedented (or 'beyond calculation'); (v.), Consider (I ii 347 may be deliberately ambiguous)
ACT, (i) that which took place, (ii) performance of part of a play, V ii 77
ACTION, (perhaps) indictment, (or) trial, (or) the part I now have to play, II i 121
ADDRESS, Prepare
ADHERES, 'what . . . adheres', what belongs to her story
ADMIRABLE, to be wondered at
ADMIRING, filled with wonder
ADO, (needless) trouble, difficulty
ADVENTURE (n.), hazard, V i 156; (v.), risk, II iii 161; dare, IV iv 451; 'of your royal presence I'll adventure . . . week', I will take the risk ('adventure' = risk in a commercial venture) of borrowing your royal presence here a week longer
ADVIS'D, 'Be advis'd', Take careful thought
AFAR, 'is afar off . . . speaks', indirectly makes himself guilty merely by the act of speaking
AFEARD, afraid
AFFAIR, affairs, business, IV iv 727; 'affairs', important business (and political) considera-

tions, I ii 23
AFFECTION, (probably) sexual desire, (or) sudden passion (such as jealousy), I ii 138; passionate love (stronger than present meaning), IV iv 473; *see* GREEDINESS, V ii 98; 'affection of', natural inclination towards, V ii 35; 'affections', *see* THOUGHT, V i 220
AFFECTS, aspires to, desires
AFFRONT, Confront
AFTER, i.e. to follow them, IV iv 655
AGAIN, back again, II i 126, V i 43
AGAINST, in time, readiness, for, IV iv 231
AGENT, *see* FACE
AIR'D, 'been air'd', lived
ALACK, 'Alack, for lesser knowledge', Oh that I knew less
ALE (i.e. bought with the proceeds of thieving)
A-LIFE, on my life, i.e. dearly
ALL, i.e. the whole truth, II i 186; 'all but what she has with her', (i.e. probably) Hermione's jewel which she was wearing when she was found (*see* V ii 32–33))
ALLAY, means of abatement
ALLOW'D, excusable, acknowledged
ALLOWING, *see* TO, I ii 185
ALTERATION, *see* PARTY, I ii 383
ALT'RING RHEUMS, catarrhs, diseases, which debilitate his mind
AMAZEDLY, in wonder and confusion
AN, 'an it like', if it please; 'an't', if it (*see* GOOD), III iii 67; 'an't like you', if it please you; 'An't please you', If it please you

ANCIENTRY, old people

ANGLE (n.), (baited) fish-hook; (v.), 'angl'd', fished (see V ii 80); 'angling', fishing (i.e. cunningly seeking to entrap you; see LINE)

ANON, soon, at once, immediately

ANOTHER, the other, IV iv 176

ANSWER (n.), 'Laid . . . answer', A charge that you must answer, something you must be held responsible for; (v.), i.e. be content to be held responsible for, I ii 83; repay, V iii 8

APACE, swiftly

APART, see PUT, II ii 13

APE, imitator

APE-BEARER, showman who travels about with a performing monkey

APOLLO, Roman god of oracles and prophecy; see JUPITER, IV iii 30

APPARENT, heir apparent, i.e. closest, I ii 177; see VISION, I ii 270

APPEAR, see DARES, II iii 56; see ENCOUNTER, III ii 48; appear so, IV iv 581

APPOINT, 'appoint myself', place myself of my own free volition

APPOINTED, 'royally appointed', equipped like royalty

APPROBATION, 'nought for approbation', needed nothing more to achieve actual proof

APPROVED, proved

AQUA-VITAE, brandy

ARGUMENT, subject-matter

ARM, i.e. power to punish, II iii 5

ART, 'art which . . . piedness shares', i.e. gardener's skill in cross-breeding which, in producing 'streaky' variegations of colour ('piedness') in flowers, rivals (or 'works with'); i.e. the means which allows Nature to improve upon herself (by grafting and cross-breeding), IV iv 91

AS, (often =) as if; as though, IV iv 184; As it would be for, V i 42; as if they were, V i 222; So that, V iii 68; 'as thou call'st him', as you (rightly) call him

ASPECT, (astrological term for the way in which, from their relative positions, heavenly bodies look upon each other and are seen by the observer on earth; see INFLUENCES)

ASSISTED WITH, accompanied by

AT, 'at friend', in the way of friendship

ATTACH, arrest

ATTEND, wait for

ATTENTIVENESS, i.e. listening to it

ATTORNEYED, performed by substitutes, deputies

AUDIENCE OF, witnessing by

AUGHT, anything, I ii 395

AUNTS, (slang) whores, loose women

AUTOLYCUS, (in Greek myth, Autolycus was the son of Mercury, the grandfather of Odysseus, and was a notorious and expert thief; see LITTER'D)

AVOID, be gone, I ii 462

AVOUCH, see TINKERS, IV iii 22; 'avouches', confirms, V ii 61

AWAKING, wakefulness

BAG, 'With bag and baggage', With all its belongings (i.e. unscathed, without having surrendered anything)

BAITS, harasses (as dogs when they are set to torment chained bears; pun on 'beat')

BALLAD, (doggerel ballads were often written on subjects of popular interest, printed on broadsheets, and offered for sale; at IV iv 253ff., Shakespeare parodies the contemporary fashion for writing ballads about marvellous happenings which were asserted to be true and to be attested by witnesses)

BALLAD-MAKERS, see BALLAD

BARBARISM, rudeness of language

BARE, bore

BARK, small sailing-boat, III iii 8, V ii 66

BARNE, child

BARRICADO, 'No barricado . . . belly', There is no way of barricading a womb

BASENESS, 'by that forced baseness', under that wrongly-imposed name of bastard

BASILISK, see SIGHTED

BASTARDS, i.e. hybrids (the streaks being caused by the crossing of different varieties of plant), IV iv 83

BAWCOCK, fine fellow (from the French 'beau coq')

BAWDY PLANET, see PLANET

BE, see SAY, I ii 298; i.e. 'prevented', I ii 405; 'being', see CHILDISH, IV iv 394; 'being done', see NOT, III ii 162

BEARD'S, (probably Antigonus's)

BEARING, 'whom, Though bearing misery . . . on him', on whom I wish to gaze once again, and for that reason desire to go on living, although my life is one of misery

BEARING-CLOTH, wrap in which a child was carried to baptism

BECOME, (often =) suit, befit; see FACE, I ii 114; 'it becomes', i.e. my confused speech befits, V i 187; 'becoming', see VESSEL

BED-SWERVER, adulteress

BEFORE, ahead, IV iv 812; go ahead, IV iv 816

BEGIN, originate, IV ii 42

BEGUILE, 'beguile nature of her custom', drive Nature out of business

BEHIND, to follow (in the future), I ii 63

BEHOVE, 'does behove . . . inform'd', would be advantageous for me to learn; 'behoves', befits

BENCH'D, 'bench'd and rear'd to worship', given an exalted official position ('bench'd') and raised to a place of honour

BEND, 'for Bohemia bend', are journeying towards Bohemia

BENEDICTION, 'a benediction', blessedness

BENEFIT, 'nothing benefit . . . reporting', in no way profit you to know or be fit for me to tell you; 'benefit of access', advantage of being allowed to visit there

BENTS, purposes

BESEECH, (often =) I beg; we beseech you, II iii 147; 'Beseech you', I beg you (i.e. to withdraw your needless self-criticism), I i 10

BESHREW, curse

BESIDES, i.e. who is near to, IV iv 788

BESPICE, 'bespice a cup', flavour a drink (e.g. wine) with spices (here 'poison')

BEST, Jesus (see YOK'D), I ii 419

BETIMES, quickly

BETTERS, 'What . . . Still betters . . . done', Whatever you do is always better than what you have done before

BETWEEN, see COME, II i 75; 'between's', between us

BIDE, dwell, insist

BILL, beak (i.e. mouth to be kissed)

BLANK AND LEVEL, aim (terms taken from shooting: 'blank' = the white spot in the centre of a target; 'level' = the action of aiming or the mark aimed ('levell'd') at)

BLEACHING, i.e. laid out to bleach or dry

BLEMISHES IN THEM, faults when I think of (or 'compare myself to') them

BLENCH, swerve (from the path of proper conduct)

BLESS, i.e. Guard, keep, IV iv 261; 'How accurs'd . . . blest', How accursed that I am proved right

BLISTER, (allusion to the belief that the utterance of a falsehood would blister the tongue)

BLOCKS, blockheads

BLOOD, 'blood look out', i.e. blush

BLOW, 'that may blow . . . too truly', (I am tormented thus) so that no biting ('sneaping') winds may blow at home and make us say 'my fears were only too justified' ('This . . .

truly'); 'blown', (probably) swollen (with the insects' stings; a kind of punishment inflicted by the Spaniards upon American Negroes and Indians)

BOASTS, (they say) he boasts

BODKIN'S, needle's

BOHEMIA, (often =) the King of Bohemia, Polixenes

BOIL'D BRAINS, addle-headed, senseless, people

BOLD, (oxlips are larger and stronger than cowslips)

BOLTED, sifted

BOND, 'very bond', prime and most powerful uniting force

BONDAGE, (i) tying up into a parcel, (ii) slavery (pun)

BOORS, peasants

BOOT (n.), see GRACE. I ii 80; see IV iv 626 and WITHOUT, IV iv 664; 'some boot', something in addition; (v.), profit, III ii 23

BORROW, see ADVENTURE

BOSOM, inmost thoughts, IV iv 555; 'bosoms', see PASTIME

BOUND (n.), boundary, III ii 49; (v.), 'bound up', i.e. clothed (metaphor from book-binding)

BOUNDLESS, uncontrollable

BOURN, boundary

BOWLING, i.e. the game of bowls (regarded by the servant as a gentle game)

BRANCH (v.), send out shoots, i.e. flourish

BRASS, (i.e. upon which an inscription could be engraved)

BRAVE, splendid, IV iv 199; V i 136

BREAK, 'break a foul . . . matter', introduce obscenity (or, 'threaten to perform a bawdy action'); 'broken delivery', disjointed account

BREAK-NECK, 'a break-neck', i.e. fatal

BREATH, 'in breath', i.e. alive

BREED, 'breed upon', develop from; 'both breed . . . rest thine', be enough to both pay for your upbringing, pretty one, and still remain yours (i.e. leave enough over to supply your needs afterwards); 'breeding', hatching, afoot, happening, I ii 374

BREEDING (n.), rearing, education, V ii 36

BRING, 'bring false generations', give birth to illegitimate children; 'bring thee . . . way', accompany you part of the way; 'bring . . . liking', get him to the point of approving; 'brought to bed of', gave birth to

BROW, 'you held a brow . . . distraction', your brow is furrowed by much anxiety; 'brows', (allusion to the popular jest that horns grew on the heads of cuckolds), I ii 119

BUDGET, (leather tool-) bag (*see* TINKER)

BUG, bugbear, bogey

BUGLE BRACELET, bracelet of tubular glass beads (usually black)

BURDEN, i.e. occupant (Polixenes), I ii 3; 'at a burden', at one birth; 'delicate burdens', delightful refrains

BUT, (often =) only; except, I ii 86, I ii 223, II i 92; *see* AFAR, II i 105; Than, III ii 23; that, III ii 28; *see* PURITAN, IV iii 40; *see* MOURN, IV iii 15; Unless, IV iv 90; Anything else except, IV iv 555; although, V i 141; 'But let him swear so, and', And if he goes so far as to swear that that is his reason for wishing to go; 'But of . . . natures', Except by those with the keenest minds; 'But that', i.e. In that, because, I ii 252; Were it not that, IV iv 10; 'but for our honour therein, Unworthy thee', (who makes himself by his actions unworthy of you) except in so far as he shares in my own royal honour (because he is my son); 'but began', had scarcely been born

BY, For, as a result of, I ii 390; *see* BASENESS, II iii 78; on, IV iv 246; standing by, V ii 2; 'by and by', soon

BY-GONE, *see* SATISFACTION, I ii 32

CADDISSES, worsted tapes for garters

CALLAT, scold

CALLS NOT, Does not need (*see* PREROGATIVE), II i 164

CAMBRICS, pieces of fine white linen

CANNOT, (i.e. entertain you as you have entertained us), I i 11

CAPABLE, 'be'st capable of', know anything about, are capable of understanding

CAP-A-PE, from head to foot

CAPARISON, *see* DIE

CARBONADO'D, scored across with a knife and broiled on charcoal

CARE, *see* MAKE, IV iv 347; 'Care not for', Do not be anxious about

CAREER, short gallop at full speed

CARRIAGE, handling

CASE, (i) predicament, plight, (ii) covering, skin (pun), IV iv 801; 'cases', lids

CAST OUT, i.e. cast the anchor into the sea to make it grip the sea bed, I ii 214

CAUGHT, charmed, III i 4

CAUSE, (i) cause (of the trouble), (ii) (perhaps) disease, II iii 3

CENSURE, judgement

CENTRE, *see* INTENTION, I ii 138; planet earth (believed, according to the Ptolemaic cosmology, to be the centre of the universe), II i 102

CEREMONY, 'I leave out ceremony', I am being discourteous (to you by ignoring you and talking apart to Perdita)

CERTAIN, certainly, I ii 362

CHAMBER-COUNCILS, 'as well My chamber-councils', and also with my intimate confidences (made in my private chamber)

CHANGE, exchange, IV iv 624; 'chang'd', exchanged, I ii 68

CHANGELING, (here) child stolen by the fairies because of its beauty (fairies were believed to steal beautiful children from their human parents and replace them with ugly and misshapen ones); *see* III iii 112, IV iv 677

CHANGES, *see* NINE, I ii 1

CHARACTER, written account of you (*see* V ii 33–34), III iii 47; hand-writing, V ii 34

CHARGE (n.), *see* LAY, II iii 96, V i 195; order, instructions, V i 162; 'To you a charge', Would be a source of (needless) expense to you; (v.), Persuade, I ii 30; order, II iii 179; 'charg'd', ordered, II iii 43; 'charg'd in honour', requested as a point of honour

CHARITY, *see* FOOTING, III iii 106

CHASE, hunt (Antigonus perhaps sees the bear and hears the hunting horn), III iii 57

CHEAP, *see* DEAR

CHEAT, rogue's trick, IV iii 115

CHEER, *see* WHAT

CHILD, girl-child, III iii 68

CHILDISH, 'being childish', when he was a child

CHILDNESS, childish behaviour

CHOUGHS, crows, jackdaws

CHURL, base rustic man (i.e. the Shepherd)

CIPHER, 'like a cipher . . . before it', like a nought, in itself worth nothing yet by its position multiplying the value of all those numbers which precede it, I multiply in value with one 'I thank you' all the many thousands of thanks which have preceded it

CIRCUMSTANCE, *see* PREGNANT, V ii 30; 'out of circumstance', without ceremony

CLAMMER, silence (to 'clammer' = (in bell-ringing) to increase the strokes of the clapper in preparation for stopping altogether)

CLAMOUR, 'Contempt and clamour', An outcry of contempt

CLAP, 'clap thyself my love', offer the hand-clasp that sealed the betrothal bargain and vowed your love for me

CLEAR'D, see IMPOSITION, I ii 74

CLERK-LIKE EXPERIENC'D, WHICH, proven to have the experience of an educated man, something which

CLIMATE (n.), region, clime, II iii 178

CLIMATE HERE, dwell in this country, V i 170

CLIPPING, embracing

CLOG, heavy block (e.g. of wood) attached to a man or beast to impede movement (often slang for 'wife', i.e. Perdita)

CLOSE (adj.), secret, hidden (it was believed that it would bring bad luck if one talked about gifts from the fairies), III iii 118; IV iv 482; (v.), come to an agreement

CLOUDED, i.e. calumniated

CLOWN, rustic, yokel

COACTIVE, 'With what's . . . coactive . . . nothing', You act in conjunction with things (i.e. fancies, dreams) which are unreal, and associate yourself with ('fellow'st') what is non-existent

COCK'S, woodcock (a proverbially foolish bird) is

COD-PIECE, see GELD

COGITATION, 'for cogitation . . . think', for the capacity to think is not present in the man who does not think (this, i.e. that my wife is 'slippery')

CO-HEIRS, joint heirs (the law of primogeniture does not apply to daughters)

CO-JOIN, see CREDENT

COLDER, 'colder . . . theme', colder than the subject of your verses is (for she is in her grave)

COLLECT MYSELF, calm down, control myself

COLLOP, small piece of meat, i.e. 'my own flesh and blood'

COLOUR, excuse, pretext, IV iv 847

COLOURING, see STAIN

COMBAT, 'by combat . . . good', prove her to be 'good' in a trial by combat

COME, 'come between', i.e. interrupt, cause you to halt in your speech, II i 75; 'come out', i.e. leave the prison, II i 121; 'Come home to', Prove true for, IV iv 639; 'came home', i.e. failed to grip the sea bed, I ii 214

COMFORT (n.), 'comfort in't, Whiles', some comfort to be had when one thinks that; (v.), see EXPEDITION; 'comforting', see DARES

COMMEND, Deliver, II ii 36; commit, II iii 181; 'Commend . . . perdition', Commend them to her service or condemn them to complete ruin; 'commended', committed, III ii 166

COMMISSION, authorisation, I ii 40; what is authorised, I ii 144

COMMIT, 'Commit . . . honour', Imprison me for performing honourable actions which you mistakenly interpret as crimes (i.e. as you did with Hermione)

COMMODITY, advantage

COMMUNICAT'ST WITH DREAMS, i.e. (perhaps) are founded upon and induce delusive dreams

COMPASS'D, 'compass'd . . . Prodigal Son', compass'd (= (perhaps) got possession of, contrived, took on tour) a puppet-show ('motion') depicting the story of the Prodigal Son

COMPLEXIONS, looks, facial expressions (of Leontes and Camillo)

CONCEIT (n.), 'conceit is soaking', intelligence, capacity to understand, is quick to absorb, i.e. notice; 'conceit . . . speed', thinking and worrying about the Queen's fate

CONCEITED, witty, clever

CONCEIVE, apprehend that, III ii 194; 'make conceive', create; 'Conceiving', Apprehending the significance of

CONCERN, see BENEFIT, IV iv 495; 'concerns more . . . avails', is of more importance than use to you

CONCLUSION, 'Of this . . . conclusion', Do not pursue this argument to its logical conclusion

CONDUIT, 'conduit . . . reigns', conduit (perhaps 'water-spout gargoyle') which has been in use for longer than the reign of many successive kings (i.e. the Shepherd, too, is weeping; possible pun on 'reigns' = 'rains')

CONJURE, 'I conjure thee . . . suit of mine', I appeal solemnly to you by all the obligations ('parts') which honourable men recognise, not the least of which is the obligation to answer this request ('suit') of mine; 'conjur'd', summoned up (as a magician summons up spirits)

CONSCIENCE, consideration, inner knowledge, III ii 44; 'In my conscience', To my mind

CONSIDER'D, rewarded, IV ii 16

CONTINUE, see FOUNDATION, I ii 430

CONTRACT, i.e. Betrothe, IV iv 382; 'contracted', engaged to be married

CONTRARY, see WAFTING, I ii 372

COP'ST WITH, have to do with

COPY (n.), image, II iii 99; 'copy out of', exact copy of

CORDIAL, restorative, heartwarming, V iii 77; 'were cordial', would be like a 'cordial' (= curative, medicinal, drink)

CORSE, corpse

COUNTED, considered to be, III iii 33

COUNTENANCE, demeanour, (or) countenances, V ii 45

COUNTERS, metal disks used in calculating

COUPLES, 'go in couples with her . . . trust her', when I travel I'll keep as close to her as if we were two hounds leashed together ('go in couples'); and I will trust her no further than I can see or touch her

COURTED, 'courted now . . . occasion', wooed (by Fortune) with a twofold opportunity (for gain)

COZEN'D, tricked

COZENERS, cheats, tricksters

CRACK (n.), flaw

CRACKS (v.), 'cracks his gorge', splits his throat

CRAM'S, cram me

CREDENT, 'Then 'tis very credent . . . something', Then it is very credible ('credent') that you will also fasten yourself upon something that is in fact real ('something')

CREDIT, belief; 'Lack I credit', Am I not believed; 'bear no credit', win no belief, not be credible

CRICKETS, i.e. the chattering ladies

CRONE, (i) withered old woman, (ii) (bleating) old ewe

CROWN-IMPERIAL, yellow fritillary

CROWNS, see EACH

CRUTCHES, 'they . . . crutches', i.e. those already very old, I i 37

CRY, 'both yourself and me Cry lost . . . goodnight', proclaim both yourself and me to be lost, and so farewell for ever

CUCKOLD'S HORN, (allusion to the fact that animal horn, when in thin sheets, is almost transparent; see BROW)

CUPBEARER, servant who serves wine

CURIOUS, demanding care

CURST, savage, fierce, III iii 124

CUSTOM, see LAW, III iv 9; see DIGEST, IV iv 12

CUT-PURSE, pickpocket

CYPRESS, a crape-like fabric

CYTHEREA'S, Venus's (Venus, the Roman goddess of Love, was said to have landed on the island of Cythera (off the South coast of Laconia) after her birth in the sea)

DAM, mother (here contemptuous, as usually used of quadrupeds), I ii 137, II iii 94; mother (unpejorative), III ii 195

DAME, mistress (of a household); 'Dame Partlet', (traditional name for a hen)

DAMNABLE, damnably

DARES, 'yet that dares . . . seem yours', yet one that dares to seem less so in this matter of condoning your evil actions (as I do not condone them) than those who seem most devoted to you (yet let you commit evil)

DASH (n.), black mark, stain

DEAD, deadly, IV iv 426

DEAL, large amount, V ii 23

DEAR, loving, loyal, II iii 149; 'Let what is dear . . . cheap', i.e. Be lavish with whatever is considered to be expensive or valuable in Sicily (as if it were cheap)

DEATHS, 'deaths in death', i.e. tortures

DEBT, see TIME

DECEMBER, i.e. a December's day

DECLIN'D, 'She had one eye declin'd . . . elevated', (proverbial) i.e. She experienced both joy and grief together

DEED, see GOOD, I ii 42

DEEM, consider

DEGREES, social ranks

DELICATE, delightful, III i 1

DELIVER, report (to Polixenes), IV iv 490; say, IV iv 551; relate, V ii 3; tell, V ii 26; 'deliver'd', i.e. of a child, II ii 24; i.e. not formally and legally transferred (as in a contract of marriage), IV iv 352

DELPHOS, (i.e. the island of Delos which possessed an oracle, was reputed to be the birthplace of Apollo, and, in Shakespeare's day, was commonly known as 'Delphos')

DERIVATIVE, 'a derivative . . . mine', something to be handed from me to my offspring

DESERTS, (Bohemia did not, in fact, possess a sea-coast)

DEUCALION, see FARRE

DIBBLE, small tool used to make holes for planting

DIE (n.), 'With die . . . caparison', Gambling ('die' = a single dice) and whoring ('drab' = whore) have reduced me to these rags ('caparison' = ornamental covering spread over a horse, and hence 'apparel')

DIFFERENCE, i.e. disparity in rank (between us), IV iv 17

DIGEST, 'Digest it . . . custom', i.e. Accept it because they have become used to it

DIGNITY, 'His dignity and duty . . . off', Having thrown off his obligations both as a prince and as a son

DILDOS, ('dildo' was a common ballad refrain, often with an innuendo, for 'dildo' = phallus)

DIS, in Roman religion, the god of the underworld, equivalent to the Greek Pluto (see PROSERPINA)

DISCASE, undress

DISCONTENTING, 'discontenting . . . strive', discontented and angry father I shall (or 'you shall') strive

DISCOVER, reveal; 'discover'd', revealed; 'discovering', revealing

DISCOVERY, disclosure (to you)

DISEASE, i.e. of being cuckolds, I ii 207

DISGRAC'D, ungraceful, disgraceful (see PLAY)

DISH'D, see TASTES

DISHONESTY, dishonourable actions

DISLIKEN, see DISMANTLE

DISMANTLE, 'Dismantle you . . . seeming', Remove your outer garment and, as far as you can, make yourself unlike your true appearance

DISPATCH, make haste

DISPUTE, discuss

DISSEVER'D, separated

DISTEMPER, ill-humour

DISTRACTION, see BROW, I ii 149; 'of such distraction', so altered by emotion

DIVERS, various, varying

DIVIDES, 'o'er and o'er divides him . . . kindness', keeps on talking in turn of his former unkindness (to Polixenes and Perdita) and his present love (for them and Florizel)

DIVINE, priest, III i 19

DO, see UNDOES, V ii 56; 'Do not', i.e. You mean, surely, you 'do not' (not 'dare not') know, I ii 377; 'does', i.e. uses, II i 73; is, fares, II iii 10; 'doing', see EACH, IV iv 143; 'As you feel doing thus', (perhaps) (i) Just as you feel me doing this (i.e. Leontes pulls Antigonus's beard or tweaks his nose), (or) (ii) Just as one can feel such an action as this (i.e. Leontes grasps one hand with another, or strikes the wall; see INSTRUMENTS); 'done', finished speaking, V i 75; 'dost', do you

DOLE, see HAPPY

DOLOUR, grief

DORICLES, (the name Florizel has assumed for his disguise)

DOUBLE, twice over, a second time, V iii 107

DOXY, female beggar (or 'beggar's wench')

DRAB, see DIE (n.)

DRAM, small amount (of liquid poison), I ii 320; small part, II i 138; a small unit of weight (i.e. a little more), IV iv 774

DRAW, 'draw in', i.e. perceive; 'drawn', see STAKE, I ii 248

DREAD, revered, I ii 322

DREAMS, fantasies, delusions, III ii 79

DUE, applicable, III ii 56

DUNGY, i.e. base

DURST, dared, II ii 50

DYING, see TONGUELESS, I ii 92

EACH, each of, II iii 35; 'Each your doing . . . queens', Everything you do, which is so distinctively and excellently yours ('singular') in every detail ('particular') makes whatever you are doing at that instant seem supreme ('Crowns . . . deeds'), so that all your actions are as sovereign as queens

EARNEST, part payment to secure an agreement (pun on 'earnest' of IV iv 631)

EASIER FOR, more open to

EBB'D, i.e. declined in quality (cf. 'Flow'd')

E'ER, i.e. at all, IV iv 771

EFFECT, 'effect your suits', achieve a successful outcome to your requests; 'effects', see LEAVING

EGGS, i.e. eggs are to each other (proverbial), I ii 130; see TAKE, I ii 161

ELEVATED, see DECLIN'D

EMBASSIES, sendings, interchanges, of ambassadors

ENCOUNTER, 'encounter so uncurrent . . . appear thus', conduct so unlawful ('uncurrent') I have transgressed ('strain'd') so as to appear thus (i.e. in a court of law and on trial for adultery); 'encounters', meetings

END, see WEIGHING, I ii 258; 'ends . . . winds', the sources of winds blowing from two diametrically opposite points of the compass (i.e. from opposite ends of the earth)

ENFOLDINGS, garments

ENOUGH, 'Enough . . . wonder', Enough to amaze you even then (when you know who I am)

ENTERTAIN, hospitably welcome

ENTERTAINMENT, *see* WHEREIN, I i 7; hospitality, I ii 111, I ii 118

EQUAL, 'Equal with wond'ring', To a degree that excites (and keeps pace with the growth of others') admiring wonder

ERE, before, I i 37, I ii 191

ESTATE, fortune, IV ii 39; affairs, IV iv 392

ETERNAL, for ever

EVEN, see PUSHES, III ii 2; just, III iii 76

EVENT, outcome

EVER, always, I ii 455

EVERY, 'every 'leven wether tods', every eleven sheep ('wether' = male sheep) yield a 'tod' (= 28 lbs) of wool

EXCHANGE FLESH, i.e. make love to

EXCREMENT, outgrowth (i.e. his false beard)

EXERCISE, i.e. that which constantly occupies (my) attention, I ii 166; habitual employment (and, perhaps, 'religious observance'), III ii 238

EXPEDITION, 'Good expedition . . . ill-ta'en suspicion', May good and speedy action ('expedition') help me, and may it help and comfort the gracious Queen, who is also involved in this affair (or 'part of Leontes's accusation'; 'theme' = (i) matter for feeling and action, (ii) accusation), but who in no way deserves ('nothing Of') Leontes's wrongly conceived suspicions

EXTEMPORE, on the spur of the moment (and without fear of the consequences)

EXTENDED, i.e. widespread (and unusually favourable)

EXTREMES, exaggerations

EXTREMITY, 'in the extremity . . . needs be', it was certainly an extreme of one or the other

EYE, *see* TINCTURE, III ii 202; 'eyes under . . . removedness', servants in my employment who are spying upon him during his absence from court; 'eyes over', spying eyes

EYE-GLASS, lens of the eye

FABRIC, construction

FACE, 'May a free face . . . agent', May wear a look of generous innocence; may derive its freedom from heartiness, from generosity, and from abundance of affection ('fertile bosom') and may well be a credit to the doer ('become the agent')

FACT, 'of your fact', guilty of such a crime as yours

FADINGS, ('Fading' was the name of a popular dance, and was often found in the refrains of ribald songs)

FAIL (n.), nonperformance, II iii 169; failure, lack, V i 27

FAIN, wish to

FAIR, i.e. legitimate, II i 150

FAITH, pledge, promise (to marry her), IV iv 35

FALLING, *see* WAFTING

FALSE, 'I am false of heart that way', I am cowardly in such matters

FANCY, love, IV iv 474

FANTASTICAL, eccentric

FARDEL, bundle (which), IV iv 696; bundle, IV iv 743

FARRE, 'Farre . . . off', Further off in kindred to me than is Deucalion (the equivalent in classical mythology of Noah, and hence the most distant ancestor of all mankind)

FASHION, 'of all fashion', of all sorts, ranks

FASTING, i.e. being empty, IV iv 591

FAULT, 'continue fault', continuing sinning

FAVOUR, (i) hospitable, affectionate, treatment, (ii) face, countenance (*see* I ii 381–382), I ii 365; facial features, V ii 46

FEATHER, (i.e. I am as easily persuaded as a feather is blown about by the slightest breath of wind)

FEATLY, nimbly

FEDERARY, accomplice, confederate

FEEDING, 'worthy feeding', valuable pasture lands (i.e. estate)

FEELING, heartfelt, IV ii 6

FEES, (allusion to the contemporary custom whereby prisoners paid fees to various legal and gaol officials on their release from prison)

FELLOW, partner, III ii 36; 'noble fellows', fellow nobles

FELLOW'ST, *see* COACTIVE

FERTILE BOSOM, *see* FACE

FESTIVAL, bought for the feast

FETCH OFF, do away with, kill (perhaps with a deliberate ambiguity, i.e. 'rescue')

FIE, (exclamation of disgust or impatience)

FILL'D, *see* VESSEL, III iii 22

FIND, experience, I ii 144; 'found', i.e. (i) found (when I want to rejoin you), (ii) found out (for the adulterous person you really are), I ii 179; 'finding', *see* PARTY

FIRE, *see* GIVE, II iii 8; *see* SHED, III ii 190

FIX'D, i.e. painted, varnished, V iii 47

FIXTURE, 'The fixture . . . in't', Her eye, though stationary, seems to move

FLAP-DRAGON'D, swallowed it as one would swallow a flap-dragon (a burning raisin floating on brandy which had to be extinguished by being swallowed)

FLATNESS, completeness, absoluteness

FLAUNTS, ostenatious finery

FLAX-WENCH, female flax-worker

FLAY'D, skinned (i.e. undressed), IV iv 628

FLIES, (i.e. utterly at the mercy), IV iv 532

FLORA, goddess of fertility and flowers

FLOW'R-DE-LUCE, fleur-de-lis, iris

FLY, flee, IV iv 757

FOND, see LEAVING, IV i 18; foolish, IV iv 418

FOOL, 'of a fool inconstant', being a fool already, (to be in addition) inconstant; 'fools', (term of endearment)

FOOT, see OCCASION, I i 2

FOOTING, 'would have lack'd footing', would (i) have been without a foothold, (ii) not have founded a charitable institution ('footing' = establishment, foundation) (pun)

FOOTMAN, i.e. footpad, IV iii 61ff.

FOR, see SEALING, I ii 337; as for, I ii 351, III ii 41, III i 59, IV iii 28; see ALACK, II i 38; To be, II ii 5, III iii 29; see PRIZE, III ii 40; i.e. to turn to the subject of, III ii 69; because, III iii 32, IV iv 86, V iii 142; 'for to', to, I ii 427; 'for because', because; 'I am for you', I am ready for you; 'for's', for his, I ii 42

FORBEAR, do not do so, V iii 80; withdraw, V iii 85

FORBID, forbidden, I ii 241

FORBIDDENLY, i.e. adulterously

FORC'D, farfetched, strained, IV iv 41

FORCE, physical strength, IV iv 366; 'of force', of necessity

FORCED, see BASENESS, II iii 78

FORE, before; before, in front of, III ii 39

FORETELLS, i.e. this implies that

FORFEND, forbid

FORK'D ONE, (i) double-dealing person (of Hermione), (or) (ii) person endowed with cuckold's horns (of Leontes himself)

FORM, 'meaner form', lower social rank

FORSWEAR THEMSELVES, repudiate with oaths charges made against them

FORTUNES, wealth, possessions, IV iv 582

FORWARD, 'forward in her breeding . . . birth', far forward in her upbringing as she is inferior to me in birth

FOUNDATION, 'whose foundation . . . his body', the foundation of which is firmly built ('pil'd') upon his settled belief and will last as long as ('continue') his body does

FOURSCORE, eightieth (probably an error for 'four and twentieth')

FRAM'D, planned

FRANKLINS, yeomen, small landowners

FREE, see FACE, I ii 112; innocent, guiltless, I ii 251, II iii 30; openly accessible, II i 194; generous, II ii 44; clear, unblemished, III ii 109; noble, IV iv 540; willing, V i 70

FREEDOM, 'in the freedom . . . knowledge', as my knowledge gives me the right to

FREQUENT TO, frequently engaged upon

FRESH, young and lovely, IV iv 543

FRIEND, see AT, V i 140

FRIENDLY, being favourable, V i 161

FRIGHT, frighten

FROM, Away, apart, from, II i 194

FRONT, see PEERING

FULFILL'D, 'Will have fulfill'd . . . purposes', Are determined to have their secret purposes fulfilled

FULL, fully, I ii 129

FURNISH'D LIKE, dressed and equipped as would befit

FURY, intense passion

GAINSAY, deny; 'I'll no gainsaying', I'll tolerate no refusal

GALL'D, made sore (by rubbing)

GALLIMAUFRY, ridiculous jumble, medley

GALLOWS, 'Gallows . . . highway', i.e. Highway robbery (in contrast to petty thieving) is too serious a crime for me to participate in, because hanging (the normal punishment for highway robbery) and 'knock' (the hard blows a highwayman may receive from his intended victim) are too prevalent

GAP, see BREAK, IV iv 194

GELD, 'geld . . . purse', cut off a purse from a 'codpiece' (a bag-like flap on the front of Elizabethan breeches)

GENERATIONS, see BRING

GENTLE, see SUCCESS, I ii 394; noble, II ii 10; i.e. 'dearest', IV iv 46; kind, generous, courteous, V ii 146; 'Gentle my', My noble

GENTLEMAN, man of 'gentle' (i.e. 'noble') birth, I ii 391; 'gentlemen born', (to be officially 'gentleman born' one had to be able to prove that one had been descended from three degrees of gentry on both sides of one's family)

GENTRY, nobility, status as 'gentlemen' (see GENTLEMAN)

GERMANE, related

GEST, stage or halt in a (royal) journey, i.e. allotted time (for that stage of his journey)

GILLYVORS, gillyflowers, clove-scented pinks

GIVE, i.e. Would I give, I ii 330; account, III ii 93; see LIE, IV iv 712, IV iv 715, V ii 127; 'Given to the fire', (death by burning was the usual punishment for high treason and 'petty treason' (= conspiracy to murder one's husband or master))

GLASS, see RUNNING, I ii 306; hour-glass (which he carries), IV i 16; mirror, IV iv 14, IV iv 589

GLIB, castrate

GLISTER, 'glistering', glistening brightness, freshness (see STALE); 'glisters', glistens, shines

GLOVES, (gloves were often perfumed), IV iv 217

GO, see COUPLES, II i 135; 'Go to', (interjection expressing disgust or remonstrance), I ii 182; 'Go to', Go on, IV iv 681; 'go right', see MOURN, IV iii 18; 'go about to', intend, wish, to, IV iv 213; 'gone', lost, IV iv 808

GOAL, i.e. point (of my speech)

GOOD, 'good deed', indeed, in very truth, I ii 42; 'Good times encounter her', May a happy issue befall her, II i 20; 'Good my', My good; 'Good luck . . . will', (God) send me good luck, if it be Thy will; 'in good time', (expression of indignation); 'good now', please, V i 19

GOODNIGHT, see CRY

GOSSIPS, baptismal sponsors, godparents (for the baby)

GOT, begot, fathered, II ii 104, III iii 72

GRAC'D, befitted

GRACE (n.), (i) seemliness, (ii) divine Grace, (iii) the girl's name 'Grace' (see I ii 99), (pun), I ii 105; 'would her name were Grace', I wish (i) the 'sister's' name were 'Grace', (ii) that it was a blessed deed (pun), I ii 99; see RUE, IV iv 76; favour, IV iv 765; 'Grace to boot', Grace in addition, i.e. Heaven help us!; 'better grace', greater honour (when I am vindicated)

GRACEFUL, full of divine grace

GRACIOUS, i.e. possessed of princely qualities, IV ii 24

GRAFTED, grown in (like a shoot in a tree)

GRANGE, farm

GRAVE (adj.), (probably) worthy, having importance, V iii 1; (n.), 'so must thy grave', so must you, now that you are in your grave

GREEDINESS, 'greediness of affection', eagerness arising from love

GREEN, immature, III ii 178

GREEN-SWARD, grassy turf

GRIEVING, see LEAVING

GROSS (adj.), palpable, manifest, II i 176; (n.), 'by th' gross', i.e. in large numbers

GROUND, reason, cause, I ii 353; 'Upon this ground', In this matter

GROW, 'How . . . grow', How could this come about; 'grew to his tunes', were so attracted by his tunes that it was almost as if they had grown especially for the purpose of hearing them

GROWTH, see UNTRIED

GUIDING SPIRIT. 'A better guiding spirit', Someone better fitted than you to look after her

GUILT, establishment of guilt

GUILTY, see UNTHOUGHT-ON, IV iv 530

GUST, taste, i.e. know of (i.e. Leontes ponders the proverbial lore that the husband is always the last to find out about his wife's adultery)

HA', Have

HABITED, clothed

HABITS, clothes, vestments

HAIR, 'all men of hair', (i.e. by dressing themselves in animal skins in order to look like satyrs)

HAL'D, Dragged

HALLOO'D, shouted

HALLOWED, blessed, holy (like holy relics)

HAMMER'D OF, shaped, worked out (i.e. deliberated upon)

HAND (n.), see THAT, III iii 5; 'hands', signatures, IV iv 277; (v.), lay a hand on, II iii 63; 'handed', was involved in

HAND-FAST, custody

HANGING, (the normal punishment for the theft of anything in excess of twelve pence in value), IV iv 617

HAPPILY, perhaps

HAPPY, propitious, I ii 363; 'happy man . . . dole', (colloquial) may it be his lot in life ('dole') to be a happy man

HARDER, 'harder bosoms', see PASTIME

HARD'NING, (i) i.e. in a frown, (ii) see BROWS

HARLOT, lewd, lascivious

HAVE, i.e. will find, III iii 66; 'Have at it', I will attempt it, IV iv 289–290; 'You have of these pedlars', There are some pedlars; 'What you have to the King', what is your business with the King; 'had', when I have received it, II i 186; Would have been, II iii 184; would have, III ii 65; 'had like to have', *see* YOUR; 'hast', have you; 'hath', have, I ii 1, I ii 199

HAVING (n.), property, IV iv 706

HE, i.e. Antigonus, II i 191; i.e. the sun, IV iv 779; 'He's', i.e. The Shepherd is, IV iv 337

HEAPING FRIENDSHIPS, piling up of kind services

HEARD, i.e. obeyed, II ii 115

HEAT, 'heat an acre', i.e. race at full speed over a short distance

HEAVINGS, deep groans or sighs

HEFTS, heavings, retchings

HENT, grasp (in order to leap over)

HER, herself, I ii 184; 'her I', i.e. the woman whom I had just, V i 62

HERE, 'They're here . . . already', i.e. People are already aware of my predicament

HERETIC, 'It is an heretic . . . in't', It will be you who make the fire that are the heretic, and not I who am burnt by it (allusion to the fact that burning at the stake was the extreme punishment for heresy)

HIGH, *see* ODDS, V i 207

HIM, a man (Polixenes), I ii 407; as the man, I ii 412; i.e. Polixenes, II iii 18

HINDER, 'which to hinder . . . me', which, if you hindered me in this respect would, although you acted out of love, be a painful punishment to me

HIS, *see* YOK'D, I ii 419

HISS, 'Will hiss . . . grave', Will hiss at me in contempt to the end of my days

HISTORY, story, drama (played on a stage)

HIT, precisely achieved

HOBBY-HORSE, loose woman

HOGSHEAD, barrel

HOLD, i.e. grip the sea bed (i.e. cause him to stay), I ii 213; consider, IV iv 422; take, IV iv 494; 'hold some counsel', be consulted a little; 'hold thee', take this, IV iv 625; 'holding', *see* MAKE, IV iv 348; 'holds', who holds, I ii 193; 'held', *see* BROW, I ii 149; 'things not so held', things which are thought to be impossible

HOME, i.e. in deadly earnest, to the finish, I ii 248; amply, fully, V iii 4

HOMELY, plain, simple, IV ii 36; (i) ugly, (ii) humble ('state' = social rank), IV iv 418

HONEST, chaste, II i 68, II i 76, II iii 70, II iii 72

HONESTY, chastity, I ii 288

HONOUR (n.), *see* CONJURE, I ii 400; *see* BUT, IV iv 428; 'Your honour . . . desires', (perhaps) If your desires are not incompatible with your honour, (ii) If your passion has not overcome your chastity; (v.), 'We honour you with trouble', i.e. Our visit, which you call an honour, is really a trouble to you

HONOURABLE, honest, II i 111

HOOK TO ME, get hold of (perhaps as, in a sea-battle, one would hook a boat with a grappling-iron)

HOPE SO, i.e. hope you are right

HORSEMAN, i.e. mounted highwayman

HORSING, 'horsing foot on foot', mounting one's foot upon that of another person and moving it up and down

HOT, *see* NOT, II iii 32; (quibble on 'a cold purse' = an empty purse, and 'hot spices'), IV iii 114; (herbs were classified into 'hot' and 'cold' according to their supposed temperatures), IV iv 104; keen, IV iv 673

HOUR, *see* TAKE, I ii 465

HOVERING, wavering

HOW, How are you, I ii 147; What do you mean, I ii 377; What, V ii 155; 'How now', Hello (or 'How are you'); i.e. Look, what is happening, III ii 144

HOXES, 'hoxes . . . behind', hamstrings honesty

HUMOUR, (aberrant, distracted) state of mind

IDLE, foolish

IF, Even if, I ii 357; 'If at home', When I am at home; 'if to be', if it can be prevented, I ii 405; 'If any be', If, indeed, there be any guilt, II ii 63

I'FECKS, In faith

IGNORANT CONCEALMENT, (i) concealment that keeps me in ignorance, (ii) concealment on pretext of ignorance, (iii) (perhaps) misguided reticence

IMAGE, statue, V iii 57

IMMODEST, immoderate, excessive

IMPARTS THIS, i.e. Prompts me to inform you of this (i.e. the reason for my action)

IMPAWN'D, as a pledge (of my good faith)

IMPORT, 'import offending', imply that I had committed some offence against you

IMPORTANCE, import, meaning, V ii 16

IMPOSITION, 'the imposition . . . ours', if, that is, the hereditary penalty imposed upon us (i.e. original sin) were set aside

IMPUDENTLY, *see* NEGATIVE

IN, on, IV iv 784, V ii 156; 'in them', i.e. (perhaps) in comparison with, in thinking of, them, V i 8

INCENSE, incite, stir up

INCERTAIN, 'devour Incertain lookers-on', i.e. destroy citizens who cannot decide between rival claimants to the throne

INCH-THICK, i.e. solid, beyond all doubt (probable allusion to 'inch-board', the thickest normal plank)

INCIDENCY, 'incidency . . . harm', harmful event you do suspect

INCIDENT, see MALADY

INCLIN'ST THAT WAY, (i.e. towards honesty)

INDUSTRIOUSLY, deliberately

INFANT, 'from an infant', from his infancy

INFECTED, see SPIDER, II i 42

INFLUENCES, (astrological term for the emanations that were supposed to spring from the stars and which were supposed to have an influence upon all life upon earth)

INJURY, see SEALING

INKLES, linen tapes

INNOCENCE, simple-mindedness, V ii 62

INSINUATE, i.e. act (or 'question you') in a subtle and indirect manner

INSTIGATION, impulse, motive for action

INSTRUMENTS, i.e. (i) Leontes's fingers, (ii) Hermione and Polixenes (see DO), II i 154

INTELLIGENCE, information

INTELLIGENCING BAWD, spying go-between (for Hermione and Polixenes)

INTELLIGENT, 'be intelligent to', inform

INTENTION, 'thy intention . . . centre', your intensity ('intention') penetrates to the core of the soul

INTERPRETATION SHOULD ABUSE, Should misinterpret

INTERPRETERS OF, commentators upon (i.e. make manifest)

IRREMOVABLE, immovable

IS, i.e. allows one to, I ii 328

ISLE, see DELPHOS

ISSUE, (often =) offspring; see THRIVING ISSUE, II ii 45; 'whose issue', that (i) the result will be that people, (ii) the offspring (of your mother's love-play), (iii) the audience (when I make my exit) ('issue' = exit) (see HISS), I ii 188; 'fair issue', legitimate offspring

IT, i.e. he, I i 33, I i 35; its, II iii 177, III ii 98

I'TH'NAME OF ME, (comic oath, cp. 'In the name of God')

JAR, tick

JOT, 'no jot', not the slightest

JOVE, Jupiter (the king of the Roman gods)

JOY, 'both joy . . . bad', the joy as well as the terror of good and bad alike (i.e. for it both makes and then unfolds error)

JULIO ROMANO, (an Italian artist who died in 1546)

JUMP HER . . . HER, (bawdy innuendo)

JUNO, in Roman religion, the wife of Jupiter and the goddess of women (see JOVE)

JUPITER, the king of the Roman gods; 'Jupiter Became a bull . . . humble swain', (allusion to the classical myths that (i) Jupiter changed himself into a bull to enable him to woo Europa, (ii) Neptune changed himself into a ram to woo Theopane, and (iii) that Apollo changed himself into a country youth and assisted in the wooing of Alcestis by Admetus)

JUSTICES, Justices of the Peace

JUSTIFIED, see WHEREIN, I i 7; confirmed, V iii 145

JUSTIFY'T, confirm it

KEEP, keep company, I ii 344; see STABLES, II i 134; 'keep upon't', inhabit it

KERNEL, seed (i.e. youngster)

KILN-HOLE, fire-hole of a kiln (a favourite gossiping-place), fireplace

KIN TO, Like

KISS, i.e. touch, fall to, V ii 206

KITES, birds of prey (of the falcon family)

KNACK, trifle, toy, knick-knack

KNOCK, see GALLOWS

KNOW, 'Know't', Be certain of it, I ii 204; 'known', acquainted, IV iv 66

KNOWLEDGE, see FREEDOM, I i 11

LA, 'La . . . hear', There, now, you hear how she talks (to Leontes)

LACE, lacing (of her stays), III ii 170

LACK'D, see TOUCH'D, II i 176

LADY MARGERY, (term of contempt, perhaps equivalent to 'Dame Partlet' (see DAME), as 'margery-prater' = hen)

LAMENTABLY, mournfully

LAND, 'land service', (i) military service on land (i.e. what was taking place on shore), (ii) the dish that was being served up on shore

LAND-DAMN HIM, (meaning unclear; perhaps (i) abuse him with rancour, (ii) damn him throughout the land, (iii) publicly proclaim him as a slanderer ('lan-dam'), (iv) thrash him unmercifully ('lam' = thrash))

LARGE, extravagant

LAST, 'At the last', Finally, at long last

LASTING, *see* WINK

LATE, recent, II i 95; recently, II iii 91

LAW, (allusion to the doctrine of the 'Unity of Time' established by some Renaissance literary theorists, which enjoined that a single play should concern itself only with events which occur within a single day), IV i 8

LAWN, piece of fine linen cloth resembling 'cambric'

LAY, 'lay . . . to your charge', apply the old proverbial saying to your case; 'Lay't so . . . charge', You may with justice accuse him of this

LEADS OR OILS, cauldrons of molten lead or oil

LEASH, *see* STRAINING

LEAVE (n.), (often =) permission; permission (*see* TINKERS), IV iii 19

LEAVING, 'Leontes leaving . . . grieving', Turning aside from Leontes – who is filled with such grief because of the results of his foolish ('fond') jealousies

LET, 'let him', allow him (to stay), I ii 41

LEVEL, mark, target shot at; *see* BLANK AND LEVEL, II iii 6

'LEVEN, *see* EVERY

LEWD-TONGU'D, foul-mouthed

LIE, 'give . . . the lie', (i) practise a deception on us, (ii) call us liars (and therefore invoke the soldiers' revenge 'stabbing steel'), IV iv 712ff.; 'Give me the lie', (if accused to his face of dishonour, a gentleman was obliged to fight to protect his honour), V ii 127–128

LIEGE, sovereign

LIEGEMAN, loyal subject

LIFE, 'for the life to come', as for life in the next world

LIGHT (n.), 'by this good light', (oath) by my eyesight; (v.), 'light upon', i.e. choose (for a wife)

LIKE (adj.), (often =) similar; *see* OCCASION, I i 1; *see* YOUR, IV iv 716; 'like to itself', i.e. in a manner appropriate to a bastard; 'Like to', In a manner appropriate to, V i 89; 'like relation', (either) (i) telling their stories too, (or) (ii) asking you too to tell your story; (adv.), likely, II ii 27, III iii 11, III iii 54, V i 49, V i 205; (v.), please, IV iv 704; 'an it like', if it please

LIKING, *see* BRING

LIMBER, limp, flabby

LIMIT, 'get strength of limit', returned to full strength through resting for the prescribed period after giving birth to a child

LINE, 'give line', allow you as much fishing-line as you want (so that you can hook yourself)

LING'RING, slow-acting

LIP, *see* WAFTING, I ii 373

LIST, listen, IV iv 533; 'list not', do not wish to

LITTER'D, 'litter'd under Mercury', born when the planet Mercury was in the ascendant (i.e. rising to prominence above the eastern horizon. The classical god Mercury was the god of thieves; in later astrology, the planet Mercury was believed to promote thievery)

LIVELY MOCK'D, realistically imitated

LIVER, 'liver . . . her life', i.e. body as diseased as is her behaviour

LIVING (adj.), i.e. who are alive, V i 147; (n.), property, estate, IV iii 92

LO, 'lo you now', i.e. now take note of this

LONELY, isolated

'LONGS, belongs

LOOK, 'look . . . wert', look favourably in your direction, III ii 211; 'Look to', Take care of, III iii 8; 'look upon the hedge', i.e. urinate; 'look'd big', put on a bold front; 'looks', looks for, IV iv 350; 'looks like sooth', gives the impression of being an honest man ('sooth' = truth)

LORDINGS, little lords

LOSING, being lost

LOSS, destruction, II iii 191; the condition of being lost, III iii 51

LOST, *see* CRY, I ii 411; 'I am lost', i.e. I die

LOUD, rough, stormy, III iii 11

LOUD'ST, 'advocate to th' loud'st', loudest advocate (as loud and vehement as I can be)

LOZEL, scoundrel (to Antigonus)

LUNES, fits of lunacy

MAKE, *see* COMBAT, II ii 60; *see* STALE, IV i 13; 'make conceive', create; 'make a care . . . holding her', are seriously concerned to keep her happy; 'makes', *see* TRIFLES, II iii 62; 'make's', make me, I ii 91; 'made', (i.e. your prosperity is assured) III iii 113; 'Made up', Added up; 'made me', made, IV iii 38

MALADY, 'a malady . . . maids', an illness most commonly suffered by young maidens (allusion to 'green-sickness', a form of anaemia suffered by young girls which can turn their complexion pale or greenish, much like the colour of the primrose. Legend had it that unmarried girls who died of this ailment were often turned into primroses)

MALICIOUSLY, violently

MAN, the man who, IV iv 788

MANKIND, masculine, unwomanly, II iii 67

MANNER, see YOUR, IV iv 717

MANNERLY DISTINGUISHMENT, fit and proper (linguistic) distinction

MANTLE, cloak, V ii 32

MARBLE, 'Who was most marble', Even the most hard-hearted

MARIGOLD, 'marigold, that goes . . . weeping', (allusion to the fact that the marigold closes its petals at sunset, and opens them wet with dew at sunrise)

MARK (n.), 'gracious mark o'th'land', one whose graces cause him to be noted by everybody; (v.), take heed of, I ii 408; observe closely, II i 65, V i 63

MARRY, Indeed (originally an oath 'By (the Blessed Virgin) Mary')

MARTED, see NOTHING

MARVEL, astonishment, V i 188; wonder, V iii 100

MASKS, (women often wore masks to protect whole or part of their faces against the sun)

MASTER, (Autolycus had once been in Florizel's service: see IV iii 13), IV iv 699

MASTERLY, masterfully, excellently

MATERIAL, 'made . . . more material', i.e. Asserted that his own affairs were more important to him

MATTER, i.e. sufficient, valid cause, I i 31; (source of) serious interest, I ii 166; substance, content, II iii 98; subject-matter (for thought), IV iv 673

MAY, that may, IV iv 616

MEAN (adj.), of low rank, V i 93; (n.), means, IV iv 89 f.; 'means', tenors, IV iii 40

MEANS (v.), i.e. by his distracted facial expressions, I ii 146

MEASURE (n.), stately stride, IV iv 721; (v.), judge, II i 114; 'measur'd', i.e. travelled across

MEDAL, 'like her medal', as if she were a miniature portrait of herself (worn in a locket around his neck)

MEDDLER, 'Money's a meddler . . . ware-a', Money has a share in everything, and puts to sale all that men have

MEDICINE, (i) restorative, (ii) physician

MEET (adj.), suitable

MEND, improve (upon); improve (i.e. to mask her bad breath), IV iv 163

MENTION'D, see I ii (Time identifies himself with the playwright – one tradition has it that the part may have been acted by Shakespeare himself)

MERCURY, see LITTER'D

MESS, group (or 'dish', 'course of dishes'); 'lower messes', inferior people ('mess' = group of people served together at a table)

METHINKS, it seems to me; 'methought', it seemed to me; 'methoughts', methought, it seemed to me (that)

MIDWIFE, (term of contempt), II iii 159

MILLINER, haberdasher, seller of gloves, ribbons, etc.

MINDED, reminded

MINE, i.e. my eyes, V i 67

MINGLE, 'To mingle . . . bloods', (perhaps an allusion to the Aristotelian notion that sexual intercourse was a mingling of bloods); 'mingle faith', join in a pledge (of marriage)

MINISTER, see TEMPT, II ii 50

MISSINGLY, aware of missing him

MISTRESS, see MORE, III ii 57

MISTRUCTED, suspected

MOCK'D, see LIVELY MOCK'D, V iii 19; counterfeited, V iii 20; 'mock'd with', fooled by, V iii 68

MOE, more

MOIETY, portion, half, share

'MONGST, among

MONSTROUS, unnatural, i.e. incredible, V i 41

MORE, again, III iii 36; 'More than mistress . . . acknowledge', I must not acknowledge that I possess (am 'mistress of') faults greater than that of which you accuse me, calling it a 'fault' (i.e. she will not acknowledge 'bolder vices', but merely her guiltless friendship with Polixenes); 'In more . . . does require', (probably) In more ways, to a greater degree, than this deed does deserve, II iii 189; 'more known', better acquainted

MORT O'TH'DEER, (perhaps) (i) the four long notes of the horn to announce the death of the deer (hunting phrase), (ii) the sighs of the dying deer

MOTION, see COMPASS'D, IV iii 91

MOURN, 'But shall I go mourn . . . go right', But shall I mourn because I am out of service, my dear? No – when I wander about (looking for things to steal) on moonlit nights, then I am living the life that is right for me

MOVE, 'mov'd', angered, I ii 150; 'moves', can move my emotions, can persuade, I ii 20; 'moving', see RIPE, I ii 332

MUDDY, i.e. disturbed in mind (as clear water

113

is muddied by being 'unsettled')

MULTIPLY, *see* CIPHER

MUST, *see* THEREABOUTS, I ii 379

MUZZL'D, i.e (perhaps) fixed into its sheath (so that it could only be a harmless ornament)

NAME, In the name of, III iii 100; 'in the name of', under the title of (i.e. he is 'Time')

NATURE, i.e. human nature (with its sense of the bonds of affection between parents and children), I ii 151; 'natures', *see* BUT, I ii 226

NAYWARD, 'to th' nayward', towards denial

NEAT, 'not neat, but cleanly', (recollecting that 'neat' is an ancient term for 'horned cattle', Leontes corrects himself; *see* BROWS)

NEAT-HERDS, cattle-herders

NEB, beak, mouth (to be kissed)

NECESSITY, 'Were there necessity . . . denied it', If there were some real need of yours behind your request, even though there were a really important reason which would make me wish to refuse

NEEDS, *see* WHAT, II iii 126

NE'ER, 'ne'er so false', as false as it could be

NEGATIVE, 'be impudently negative . . . thought', shamelessly deny that you can see, hear, or think

NEIGHBOUR (v.), *see* PLACES, I ii 449

NEPTUNE, Roman god of the sea (*see* JUPITER)

NEXT, nearest, I i 195; nearest, shortest, III iii 118ff., III iii 121f.

NIGH, near

NINE, 'Nine changes . . . note', The shepherd has been able to record the waxing and waning ('changes') of the moon nine times (i.e. nine months have passed)

NO, not (*see* TO), I ii 362; 'no thought of him', let me not think of him (Polixenes)

'NOINTED, anointed, covered

NONE, *see* 'TIS, IV iv 807; 'I'll none of you', I will have nothing to do with you; 'We'll none on't', We'll have nothing to do with it

NOR, 'If word nor oath', If neither word nor oath; 'nor . . . nor . . .' neither . . . nor . . .; *see* NEGATIVE, I ii 275

NOT, are not, II iii 107; do not, IV iv 464; *see* WOMEN, V i 109; 'Not so hot', i.e. Don't be so hasty; 'with death . . . Not doing it and being done', threatened him with death if he did not do it and encouraged him with the promise of reward if he did do it

NOTE, *see* NINE, I ii 2; distinction, IV ii 41; *see* OUT, IV iii 43; 'came into my note', came under my observation; 'notes of admiration', marks of wonder (or 'exclamation marks')

NOTHING, *see* EXPEDITION, I ii 459; not at all, IV iv 343, V iii 28; in no way, not at all, IV iv 495; nonsense (perhaps pun on 'noting' = tune), IV iv 602; 'nothing marted', done no business; 'concerns him nothing', is of no importance to him

OCCASION, *see* COURTED, IV iv 819; 'on the like occasion whereon . . . on foot', in similar circumstances and for similar reasons to those which at present cause my services to be engaged ('on foot' = in action, in motion)

ODD, 'odd shilling', a few shillings; 'The odds for . . . alike', (perhaps) (i) prince and shepherdess are equally at the mercy of Fortune (ii) the odds on the union in marriage of those of high and low social status are the same as that of the stars 'kissing' the valleys, (iii) the odds of high and low numbers coming up in the game of dice that is life are the same

O'ER-DY'D BLACKS, black (perhaps 'mourning-') clothes (i) dyed another colour (i.e. their colour, and the fidelity of their owner, is false), (ii) dyed with too much dye (and hence make weak and unwearable by the acid used in black dye)

O'ERWEEN, am conceited enough

OF, in, I i 32; by, I ii 226; By (or 'From'), I i 387, III ii 4; for, II iii 149; *see* FOOL, III ii 183; 'of these pedlars', *see* HAVE

OFFEND, offends

OFFER, dare, presume, IV iv 765

OFFICE, service, IV iv 563; 'The office', i.e. That duty, II ii 31; 'offices', kindly services, II iii 188; kindnesses, V i 149

OFFIC'D, *see* STAND

OFFICIOUS, (perhaps) ready to do kind offices, II iii 158

ON, *see* OCCASION, I i 1f.; In consequence of, II ii 22; about, III iii 78; 'On thy soul's . . . torture', On peril of damnation to your soul and torture to your body; 'On his shoulder, and his', Now at one man's shoulder, now at another's; 'on's', of us, I ii 206; of his, IV iv 742; 'on't', of it; *see* NONE, IV iv 325

ONE, i.e. misery, affliction, IV iv 561; *see* YOUR, IV iv 716; *see* EXTREMITY, V ii 19

OPEN, reveal, IV iv 727

OPPOSE, (should) oppose himself; 'opposed', *see* END, I i 28

OR . . . OR . . ., either . . . or . . .

ORDER, *see* PASS

O'TH'SUN, sun-dried

OUR, (often =) my (Polixenes, Leontes, and Florizel often use the royal plural)

OUT, *see* COME, II i 121; i.e. dislocated, IV iii 70; (expression of mild scorn), IV iv 110; *see* CIRCUMSTANCE, V i 90; 'O, I am out', Oh, I am wrong; 'out of my note', not on my list

OUTSIDE, i.e. clothes, IV iv 622

OVER, *see* SWEAR, I ii 424; i.e. superior to, IV iv 90; *see* EYE, IV iv 644

OVERTURE, public disclosure

OWE, own

OW'D, *see* SINCE

OWN IT, i.e. acknowledge its applicability, III ii 57

OXLIPS, (a natural hybrid of the cowslip and the primrose; *see* BOLD)

PACE, proceed, IV i 23

PADDLING, 'But to be paddling . . . fingers', But (it is not becoming) for a lady to be fondly fingering a gentleman's palm and pinching his fingers

PAINTED, i.e. with cosmetics

PAINTING, paint

PALE, (i) domain, bounds, (ii) paleness, IV iii 4

PANDAR, (immoral) go-between

PANTLER, pantry servant

PARCELS OF CHARGE, valuable articles

PART (v.), 'part the time between's', i.e split the difference (of one week) between us

PARTAKE, drink, consume, II i 41; 'Partake to', Share with

PARTING, *see* WHOSE

PARTS, duties, obligations (*see* CONJURE), I ii 400

PARTICULAR, 'particular thrifts', personal gains

PARTY, person (being), III ii 2; participant, person involved, IV iv 800; 'I must be A party in . . . alter'd with't', my looks, too, must have changed, reflecting the altered position in which I find myself (or 'I must be a cause of this alteration (in the king's manner and your own) since I find myself affected in this way by it'); 'parties', allies, supporters, II iii 21

PASH, 'rough pash', shaggy (bull's) head (*see* BROWS)

PASS, 'to pass it', by letting it pass; 'Let me pass . . . receiv'd', Accept me as the same as I always was ('same I am' – Time uses the present tense because he stands outside time) before the oldest injunctions ('order' – *see* LAW) became established, or before those things came about which are now accepted as a rule ('receiv'd'); 'passes', *see* STAIN, II ii 19

PASSAGE, 'in whose . . . passage', (i.e. a threat of torture as well as death)

PASSING, exceedingly

PASTIME, 'a pastime . . . bosoms', source of mirth to those who have less tender hearts; 'make their pastime at', derive amusement from

PATE, head

PATTERN, match, show a precedent for, III ii 34; 'By th' pattern . . . his', (image taken from dressmaking: i.e. their thoughts are as identical to each other as a piece of cloth cut out to make a garment is an exact copy of the pattern by which it was cut)

PAWN, venture, hazard, II iii 165

PAY, (i.e. in self-criticism), I i 15; 'May be he has paid you more', (i.e. fathered an illegitimate child by you); 'paid home', amply, fully, repaid

PEER, appear (or 'peep out'); 'Peering . . . front', Appearing at the beginning of April

PEERLESS, without equal

PENNYWORTH, i.e. bargain

PERCHANCE, Perhaps

PERDITA, i.e. 'The Lost One' (from the Latin)

PERDITION, *see* COMMEND

PERFECT, certain, III iii 1

PERIL, 'on . . . peril, and on mine', at the risk of incurring your anger and my own

PERPETUITY, 'for perpetuity', *see* TIME

PERSON, 'As 'twere . . . person', i.e. Just as if he were your father

PERSONAL, make in person

PERTINENT, apt, apposite

PETITOES, pigs' trotters (i.e. 'feet')

PETTY, minor

PHEASANT, (the Clown confuses 'royal court' and 'legal court', and assumes that he and his father are expected, as was often the case, to bring a bribe of a pheasant to the Justice of the Peace), IV iv 731

PHOEBUS, Phoebus Apollo (*see* PRIM-ROSES)

PHYSIC (n.), Medicine

PHYSICS (v.), 'physics the subject', acts as an invigorating medicine, cordial, to the nation

PICKING ON'S TEETH, picking of his teeth (allusion to the fact that it was fashionable for gentlemen to use toothpicks, and wear them as ornaments)

PICTURE, (sculpted) image, V ii 166; 'in picture', (perhaps) in appearance

PIECE (n.), masterpiece, person, IV iv 32; masterpiece, work of art, V iii 38; 'piece of earth', mortal (perhaps 'masterpiece of humanity'); (v.), augment, add to, V ii 105; 'piece up in himself', i.e. add to his store of grief within himself

PIEDNESS, see ART

PIL'D, see FOUNDATION

PIN AND WEB, (disease of the) cataract

PINCH'D, (perhaps) tormented, manipulated, II i 51

PLACES, 'thy places . . . mine', i.e. your position will always be to be close to my throne

PLACKET, petticoat (or the slit in a petticoat, hence 'pudendum'); 'wear their plackets . . . faces', toss their petticoats over their heads (or display ('wear') their petticoats as openly as they display their faces, i.e. disclose their most private affairs (see above)

PLAIN, simple, honest, IV iv 710; smooth (Autolycus wilfully misunderstands the Clown), IV iv 711

PLANET, 'It is a bawdy planet . . . predominant', It is like a bawdy planet which will 'strike' (astrological term = 'destroy by malign influence', i.e. 'spread ruin') whenever it is 'predominant' (astrological term = 'in the ascendant', i.e. just above the eastern horizon and rising towards its zenith); 'ill planet', (see above)

PLANT, establish

PLAY, play with, II i 52; 'Go, play, boy, play . . . part', Go and play, child; for your mother is engaging in love-play, and I too am acting a part, but so ungraceful and disgraceful a part (i.e. the role of the stupid, complaisant, husband) (pun on 'play' = (i) amuse oneself, (ii) engage in amorous love-play, (iii) act a theatrical role; see ISSUE)

PLEASANT, merry, funny, IV iv 188

PLEASE, If it pleases, II ii 46; 'Please you', Be so good as to; 'So please you', If it pleases you

PLIGHT, (i.e. her pregnancy), II i 118

PLUCKING, see STRAINING

POINT YOU FORTH, direct you

POINTS, tagged laces used for fastening the 'hose' to the 'doublet', etc. (pun on 'points' = legal arguments)

POKING-STICKS, metal rods used to iron fluted ruffs

POMANDER, scent-ball

POMP, 'pomp . . . glean'd', high social and material standing which I can win there

PONDEROUS, weighty, important

POOR, trivial, III ii 186

POST (n.), (allusion to the fact that public notices were pinned up on posts in Shakespeare's day), III ii 99; haste, II i 182; 'posts', speedy messengers

POSTERNS, back gates (in the city walls)

POWER, 'to my power', to the best of my ability

PRACTICE, see UNCLASP'D

PRACTIS'D, studied

PRANK'D UP, bedecked

PRAY, I pray, beg, II ii 6

PREDOMINANT, see PLANET

PREFERMENT, advancement (to some office of authority)

PREFIX'D, Preordained

PREGNANT, 'pregnant by circumstance', made clear by detailed (circumstantial) evidence

PREPOSTEROUS, (Clown's mistake for 'prosperous')

PREROGATIVE, 'our prerogative . . . counsels', My royal prerogative frees me from any obligation to consult you

PRESENCE, see ADVENTURE, I ii 38

PRESENT (adj.), (often =) immediate; imminent, immediate, III iii 4; see EACH, IV iv 145; 'without My present vengeance taken', without my immediately avenging such a calamity; (n.), present instant, time, I ii 192; see STALE, IV i 14

PRESENTLY, immediately

PRESSES, 'presses . . . sleep', i.e. weighs upon him and prevents him sleeping

PRETENCE, purpose, design

PRIEST, see WHERE, IV iv 450

PRIG, thief

PRIMROSES, 'primroses, That die . . . strength', (the primroses are seen as dying 'unmarried' because their flowers die in early spring before the sun (seen as 'Phoebus', the classical sun-god, and as the flowers' bridegroom) has reached manhood (i.e. its full summer strength))

PRINCIPAL, 'But with . . . principal', Except if she were to share that knowledge with her most vile partner in sin ('principal' = person most responsible for a crime)

PRINT (n.), (i.e. Paulina likens the baby to a book made as a miniature copy of her father, also seen as a book), II iii 98; (v.), 'print . . . off', i.e. make an exact image of your father

PRITHEE, beg, pray you

PRIVY TO, cognisant, in the secret, of

PRIZE (n.), booty, something to be taken, IV iii 30; (v.), value, IV iv 367; 'For life, I prize . . . spare', As for life, I value it as highly as I value ('weigh') grief, which I would happily do without ('spare')

PROCESS, (legal term for the working-out of a case at law)

PROCESS-SERVER, sheriff's officer who serves summonses (similar to a bailiff)

PROCLAIM'D, see WHOSE, V i 160

PROFESS'D, made professions of friendship

PROFESSION, avowed occupation (i.e. thieving)

PROFESSORS ELSE, people who professed other faiths, worshipped other deities

PROGNOSTICATION, weather forecast in an almanac

PROMIS'D, (i.e. to marry you), IV iv 233

PROOF (adj.), 'proof against', invulnerable to

PROPER, own

PROPHECY, i.e. in calling you 'Fortunate'

PROSERPINA, 'O Proserpina . . . Dis's waggon', (allusion to the classical myth that Proserpina, the daughter of Zeus and Demeter, was gathering flowers when Dis (god of the underworld) saw her and carried her off to the underworld in his chariot to make her his queen (Demeter eventually persuaded Zeus to order Dis to allow Proserpina to return to the upper world every alternate six months); 'waggon' = chariot)

PROVE, (often =) turn out to be; test, I ii 443; 'prove so', be found to be such a one (Autolycus may be secretly alluding to his dexterity as a pickpocket)

PROVERB, (e.g. '(He is) your eldest Son, Sir, but he is so like you that he is the worse for it')

PUBLISH'D, publicly denounced

PUGGING, 'set my pugging . . . edge', sharpens, makes keen ('set on edge') my appetite ('tooth') for thieving ('pugging' – stealing linen put to dry was a favourite pastime of petty thieves)

PURBLIND, quite blind

PURGATION, exculpation from guilt

PURITAN, 'but one Puritan . . . hornpipes', there is only one Puritan among them, and he (is so jolly that he) sings solemn psalms to the tunes of hornpipes (lively dance tunes) (perhaps a mild jibe at the Puritans' disapproval of singing and dancing, and their alleged habit of intoning psalms in a high nasal voice – i.e. this particular Puritan sings Alto or Treble)

PUSH (n.), 'upon this push', (probably) at this moment of stress

PUSHES (v.), 'Even pushes . . . heart', Strikes even at my heart

PUT, see BLOW, I ii 14; 'Than you can put us to't', Than whatever test of that sort you can put on me; 'put on', wear (see FACE), I ii 112; 'puts forth', shows itself; 'put apart', dismiss; 'put you out', interrupted your speech; 'puts to', goes to it (i.e. copulates), I ii 277

PUTTER-ON, instigator, inciter

QUALIFY, appease; 'qualified', tempered, constituted

QUEENS, see EACH, IV iv 146

QUESTION (n.), conversation, talk, IV ii 46; 'Make that thy question . . . rot', i.e. If that is to be your line of argument ('question'), go and be damned; 'in question', under examination

QUESTION'D, 'I am question'd . . . chance', My fears raise questions in me about what may be happening

QUICK, alive ('corse' can refer to a living, as well as a dead, body), IV iv 132

QUOIFS, coifs, tight caps

RACE, root, IV iii 43

RAISE, rouse

RARE, uniquely pleasant, III i 13; unique, III i 20; 'None rare', Nothing remarkable; 'rarer', more exquisite

RARELY, exceptionally

RASH, quick-acting

REAR'D, see BENCH'D, I ii 314

REASON, It is reasonable that, IV iv 398

REASONABLE, requiring the exercise of reason, IV iv 390

REBELLION, 'in rebellion . . . so too', being in rebellion against his true, worthy, sane self, wants all his subjects to follow him and do the same

RECEIVE, 'Do not receive affliction . . . petition', Do not let my petition to heaven for vengeance (or 'my urging you to despair')

bring suffering upon you; 'receiv'd', *see* PASS, IV i 11

RECOIL, go back (in memory)

RECREATION, diversion, pastime

RED, flushed, IV iv 54

RED-LOOK'D, flushed (*see* TRUMPET)

REHEARSE, narrate

REITERATE, *see* WHICH

REJOICE, rejoice that

RELISH, *see* WHICH; 'relish'd', had a pleasing taste, found acceptance

REMEDY, 'No remedy but you will', For you must of necessity eventually marry

REMEMBER, remind, III ii 227

REMEMBRANCE, *see* ROSEMARY, IV iv 76; (you do not take pity on the) perpetuation (through an heir), V i 25

REMOV'D, *see* FETCH OFF, I ii 335; 'removed', remote, V ii 101

REMOVEDNESS, *see* EYE

REPLENISH'D, complete, consummate

REPORTING, *see* BENEFIT

REQUIR'D, deserved, III ii 61

RESORT, visiting

RESPECTING, in comparison with

REST, *see* BREED, III iii 49

RESTRAINING . . . REQUIR'D, holding it back from its proper course

RETIRED, absent, IV ii 30

REVENUE, 'my revenue . . . silly-cheat', my income is derived from 'silly cheat' (perhaps = (i) petty swindling, (ii) cheating the simple; *see* GALLOWS)

REVOLTED, i.e. unfaithful

RICH PLACE, *see* CIPHER, I ii 7

RICHER, 'No richer than', Taking nothing with him except

RICHLY NOTED, abundantly well known

RIDE, 'rides', which rides (at anchor); 'ride's', (i.e. You will get more from us with kindness than you ever would with harsh treatment)

RIFT, split

RIGOUR, tyranny

RIPE, 'ripe moving', ample, mature, considerations which persuade me

ROSEMARY, (symbolic 'remembrance' = friendship)

ROUNDING, whispering

ROUNDS, grows round-bellied (i.e. with child)

RUE, (symbolic of 'grace', i.e. repentance)

RUNNING, 'The running . . . glass', As long as it takes for the sand in an hour-glass to run out

SAD, serious, IV iv 304

SALTIERS, (servant's mistake for 'Satyrs', or, perhaps, a word meaning 'leapers', from 'sault' = jump. Dances of Satyrs were common; on 1 January 1611 an antimasque dance of ten or twelve satyrs formed part of Ben Jonson's *The Masque of Oberon* which was performed before King James and his court in London. 'One three . . . danc'd before the king' may imply that some or all of the dancers of the masque in *The Winter's Tale* had danced before the King in reality in Jonson's play)

SANCTITY, 'very sanctity', sanctity itself

SAP, vitality, i.e. promise of success

SATISFACTION, 'this satisfaction . . . proclaim'd', we heard this good news yesterday

SATISFY, (Leontes interprets the word in a sexual sense), I ii 233f.; 'satisfied', free from doubt

SAVOUR, stench, I ii 421; scent, IV iv 75

SAVOURS, tastes

SAY, 'Say it be', Suppose it is (dangerous); 'said', spoken, III ii 197

SCAPE, (sexual) escapade, III iii 69

SCARCE, scarcely, II i 99, III ii 23

SCENE, play, IV i 16; theatrical performance, IV iv 585

SCION, a shoot from grafting

SCOUR, hurry along

SEALING, 'for sealing . . . tongues', silencing, preventing, harmful talk

SECOND, 'be second to', support

SECT, religious sect

SEE, 'seeing', what he saw, V ii 16; 'seest thou', do you hear

SEEDS, (allusion to the contemporary belief that all material substance derived from 'seeds'; i.e. Florizel envisages all present and all potential life on earth being destroyed)

SEEM, 'seeming', *see* WHICH, II i 166; 'seems', *see* STALE, IV i 15

SEEMING (n.), appearance, colour, IV iv 75

SEIZ'D, 'seiz'd His wish'd ability', i.e. reduced his strength to less than he would wish it

SELF-BORN, self-same (and which I myself, as 'Time', have created)

SENSE, senses, III i 10; *see* SETTLED, V iii 72

SENSELESS, insensible

SESSION, judicial trial, II iii 201; sitting or meeting of a court of law, IV iv 674; 'sessions', trial (collective plural)

SET, plant, IV iv 100; *see* PUGGING, IV iii 7; 'set down', i.e. resolved upon

SETTLED, 'No settled . . . world', No calm sanity in the world
SEVERAL, different, I ii 438; a good many, IV iv 183
SEVERALS, separate individuals
SEV'NIGHT, seek
SHALL'S, Shall we
SHAME US, see WHEREIN
SHARES, see ART
SHARPEST, most bitter, painful
SHE, see WHAT, I ii 44; i.e. Hermione, II i 139; i.e. Perdita, V ii 74
SHED, 'shed water . . . don't', wept tears while standing in hell-fire before he would have done it
SHEEP-COTE, sheep-house
SHEEP-WHISTLING, whistling after sheep (i.e. sheep-tending)
SHEETS, i.e. marital bed, marriage, I ii 327
SHOOTS, i.e horns (see BROW)
SHORE THEM, put them ashore
SHOVELS, see WHERE
SHREW, Beshrew, curse
SHREWDLY, grievously
SICILIA, (often =) the King of Sicilia
SIGHT, see TOUCH'D, II i 176
SIGHTED, 'Make me not sighted . . . basilisk', Do not make me out to have a gaze like that of the basilisk (a mythical creature, half cock and half serpent, whose glance was supposed to be able to kill)
SILLY-CHEAT, see REVENUE
SINCE, ago, II iii 194; 'since you ow'd . . . do now', when you were my age
SINGULAR, see EACH
SINGULARITIES, rarities, curiosities
SIR'S, 'my sir's', i.e. the Clown's
SITTING, conference
SIZES, (i.e. kinds)
SKILL, see WHICH, II i 166; reason, cause, IV iv 152
SLACKNESS, i.e. in 'offices' towards him
SLAUGHTERS, see TONGUELESS
SLEEP, 'is sleep', i.e. allows one to sleep in peace, I ii 328
SLEEPY, sleep-inducing
SLEEVE-HAND, wristband
SLIP, cutting; 'slips', cuttings
SLIPP'D, i.e. sinned
SLIPPERY, i.e. unchaste, unfaithful
SLUIC'D, i.e. adulterously made love to (as water is drawn from a pond by means of a sluice)
SMACKS, tastes, savours

SMELL, smell out, i.e. understand, II i 151
SMUTCH'D, smudged, made dirty
SNEAPING, see BLOW
SO, see PLEASE, II iii 196; i.e. fact, a genuine vision, III iii 39; i.e. do the same as you imagine Hermione doing, V i 62; 'so it is', as things are; 'so that', provided that, II i 9; 'so were I', provided that I were; 'So please you', If you would be so kind as; 'So like you 'tis the worse', So like you that she is the worse for it; 'so be blest my spirit', i.e. and may my spirit only be blessed if I keep this promise
SOAKING, see CONCEIT
SOCIETY, companionship, I i 24
SO-FORTH, i.e. 'such-and-such', 'so-and-so' (Leontes avoids saying 'cuckold')
SOFT, wait, IV iv 384
SOFTLY, gently, IV iii 69ff.; slowly, IV iii 107
SOLELY, alone
SOME, a little, I ii 108; around, roughly, II i 145; i.e. sometimes on, III iii 20
SOMETHING, (often =) somewhat, a little; Somewhat (i.e. a great deal), IV iv 398; 'something gently consider'd', given a gentlemanly (i.e. generous) consideration (i.e. bribe)
SOMETIME, Something or other, I ii 254
SON O'TH'KING'S, see MENTION'D
SOOTH, see LOOK, IV iv 17; In truth, IV iv 339; 'Very sooth', Truly, indeed; 'Good sooth', In truth
SORE, heavily, thickly, (as of paint)
SORROW, mourning, penitence, V i 2
SOVEREIGNLY, 'So sovereignly . . . honourable', Who is supremely, royally, honourable
SPARE, see PRIZE (v.), III ii 41
SPEAK, see TWO, IV iv 39; 'spoke', spoken, asserted, III ii 67
SPEED (n.), see CONCEIT, III ii 142; (v.), fare, flourish, III iii 46; 'speed us', make us prosper; 'sped', flourished
SPICES, i.e. slight foretastes, III ii 181
SPIDER, (allusion to the belief that if there was a spider in the food or drink it would poison the person who consumed it, but only if he was aware that the spider was there), II i 40
SPIRITS, vital forces, V iii 41
SPLIT'ST, i.e. destroyest
SPOUTS, i.e. of tears
SPRINGE, snare
SPUR, i.e. encourage, hasten (me in my course of action), II i 187
SQUAR'D, ruled, regulated, III iii 41; 'squar'd me to', let myself be governed by

SQUARE, square piece of material covering the breast

SQUASH, unripe pea-pod (i.e. 'youngster')

SQUIER, 'by th'squier', by the square (= foot-rule), i.e. 'precisely'

SQUIRE, see STAND, I ii 171; country gentleman, landed proprietor, III iii 110

STABBING STEEL, (see LIE)

STABLES, 'I'll keep my stables . . . wife', (perhaps) I'll guard ('keep') my wife as I guard my horses (i.e. 'I'll keep my wife away from other men as carefully as I keep my mares from my stallions in my stables')

STAIN, 'to make no stain . . . colouring', to try to make something stainless appear to be stained that it goes beyond 'colouring' (= (i) the art of dying with colours, (ii) excusing)

STAIR-WORK, secret use of stairs; 'stair-work . . . behind-door-work', (i.e. methods by which the lover secretly reached his beloved and made love to her)

STAKE, 'the rich stake drawn', the high stake won by the winner (possible bawdy innuendo on 'stake')

STALE, 'make stale . . . seem to it', shall make the glistening freshness and brightness ('glistering') of the time seem stale, just as my present tale seems stale by comparison with the 'glistering present'

STAMPED COIN, good current money

STAND, make a stand, fight, III ii 43; Be, remain, IV iv 52; left there, IV iv 773; 'More monstrous standing by', in the presence of (i.e. in comparison with) others more monstrous; 'stand upon', value, set store by; 'So stand this squire . . . me', Just such a function does the boy play in my household (allusion to the role played by 'squires' (young men of good birth who served as attendants upon knights) in royal households)

STAR, (allusion to the astrological belief that the configuration of the heavenly bodies could influence the lives of men), I ii 363

STARR'D, 'Starr'd most unluckily', Born under a most unlucky star

STATE, social rank, IV iv 418; 'Of your . . . take care', Have a proper care for your high station

STAY, delay, I ii 9; wait, IV iv 334

STEEP'D, immersed (in the drink; see SPIDER)

STILL, (often =) always; always, for ever, III iii 119

STIR, move (adequately atone for), III ii 206

STOCK, plant onto which a 'scion' is grafted (see SCION)

STOMACHERS, ornamental chest-covers (to fill in the front opening of the bodice)

STRAIGHT, (often =) immediately

STRAIN'D, see ENCOUNTER

STRAINING, 'More straining on . . . unwillingly', i.e. (Like a hound) all the more eager to run forwards for the fact that my master holds me back; not lagging behind and having to be dragged along by my leash

STRAITED, hard pressed

STRANGELY, 'strangely . . . place', as a stranger to a foreign place

STRETCH-MOUTH'D, wide-mouthed

STRIKE, see PLANET, I ii 201; strike up, V iii 98

STRONG, see TELL, I ii 34

STRONGER, 'stronger blood', i.e. the passions of maturity

STUCK IN EARS, became (the sense of) hearing

STUDIED, i.e. carefully considered and prepared

STUFF'D SUFFICIENCY, fully qualified for the office

STUMBLE, (i.e. err in what she does)

STUPIFIED, see WHICH

SUBJECT, see PHYSICS, I i 36

SUCCESS, 'In whose success . . . gentle', In succession from whom we are 'gentle' (= noble)

SUCH, see DARES, II iii 57

SUDDENLY, at once

SUFFER, admit of, IV iv 517; endure, allow, IV iv 817

SUIT, request; 'suits', see EFFECT

SUP, (perhaps 'sate their 'greediness' by feasting their eyes upon the statue')

SUPERSTITIOUSLY, (perhaps 'punctiliously', or 'against accepted Protestant doctrine')

SURPRIS'D, overwhelmed

SWAIN, (rustic) youth

SWEAR, (swearing was held by some to be the prerogative of gentlemen), V ii 153; 'Swear his thought over', Though you should swear his thought to be untrue; 'I'll swear for'em', I'll be sworn do; 'be sworn', i.e. swear (that it is as innocent as she is)

SWEET, pleasant part, IV iii 3; perfumed (gloves were often perfumed), IV iv 217, IV iv 245; 'sweeter . . . Juno's eyes Or', i.e. sweeter to behold than the lids of Juno's eyes and sweeter to smell than (see JUNO)

SWERVE, (i.e. drawn by his fairness to admire him)
SWORD, (probably because the handle of a sword, when held point down, resembled a cross), II iii 167

TABLE-BOOK, notebook
TABOR, small drum
TAKE, receive (or perhaps 'delight', 'charm'), I ii 40; captivate, charm, III ii 35; bewitch, enchant, IV iv 119; 'take eggs for money', (proverbial) i.e. allow yourself to be paid in eggs (apparently cheap in Shakespeare's day) rather than money (i.e. be fobbed off with something of inferior value); 'To take the urgent hour', Seize this urgent opportunity; 'Take your patience to you', Arm yourself with patience; 'take in', conquer, subdue; 'taken', comprehended, I ii 222; see PRESENT, I ii 281; see YOUR, IV iv 716; 'takes up with', (i) swallows up, (ii) rebukes
TALEPORTER, i.e. rumour-carrier
TALL, 'tall fellow of thy hands', valiant fellow in a fight
TARDIED, delayed
TASTES, 'I know not how it tastes . . . how', I do not know what it tastes like, and would not know even if it were served up before me so that I could taste it
TAUGHT'T, taught him
TAWDRY-LACE, bright silk neckerchief (so-called after Saint Audrey whose feast was celebrated with a fair at which showy articles of dress were sold)
TELL, count, IV iv 184; 'To tell . . . strong', To say that . . . would be a strong reason
TEMPT, try, put to the test, V i 73; 'tempt . . . honour', solicit any person of standing to undertake it
TENDER (adj.), young, III ii 193; (v.), lead, IV iv 783
THAN, see COUPLES, II i 136; than that, II i 149
THAT, so that, I i 26; if, I ii 84f.; as, I ii 263; 'that to', it produces as a result, I ii 145; 'do that', i.e. kill Hermione (and/or the King of Bohemia), I ii 311; 'that we have in hand', what we are doing; 'That wilt', Because you will, II iii 109
THE WHICH, which, IV iv 553
THEM, i.e. (probably) the rules of the 'law' (see LAW), IV i 12
THEME, see EXPEDITION, I ii 459; see COLDER, V i 100

THEN, i.e. if you do indeed shun her, V iii 106
THENCE, i.e. not present there, V ii 106
THERE, i.e. at court, IV iv 725
THEREABOUTS, ''Tis thereabouts . . . you dare not', That (i.e. that you know but dare not tell me), or something like it, must be the case; for you cannot be saying that you dare not communicate to yourself what you already know, because you know it already
THEREAT, see POMP
THEREON, 'thereon . . . sworn', upon whom the King has sworn the verdict of execution
THERETO, and, in addition, I ii 391
THESE, 'these seven years', i.e. for a very long time (proverbial; see YOUR)
THEY'RE, see HERE, I ii 217
THICK, 'thick my blood', make me melancholy
THICKER, more opaque
THING, 'O thou thing . . . place', Oh you 'thing' – for I will not call a creature of your rank by the name you deserve
THINK, see COGITATION, I ii 272; 'think it', be assured of it, I ii 202; 'I think Camillo', i.e. You are Camillo, I think; 'as thought on', in accordance with his high estimation of them
THIS, This is, V iii 149
THOROUGH, Through, III ii 168
THOUGHT, 'With thought . . . affections', Recalling how it felt to feel such passions (of love as I feel)
THREATEN, see NOT, III ii 161
THREE-MEN SONG-MEN, i.e. singers of secular part-songs for treble, tenor, and bass male voices
THREE-PILE, the most costly kind of velvet
THRIFTS, see PARTICULAR
THRIVING ISSUE, successful outcome
THRONG, form a crowd and argue
THROUGHLY, thoroughly, fully
THUS, i.e. I shall say as follows, III ii 26
THWACK, 'We'll thwack . . . distaffs', We (women) will beat him on his way with our distaffs (= wooden staves upon which flax or wool would be wound before being spun; these eventually became symbolic of women's authority)
TIME, see GOOD, II i 20; 'Time as long again . . . debt', In addition, another stretch of time of the same length (nine months) should be spent by me in thanking you, my brother; and yet I should still go away in debt to you for ever; 'in good time', (an expression of indignation), IV iv 163

TINCTURE, 'Tincture . . . eye', Colour to her lip or lustre to her eye

TINKERS, 'If tinkers . . . avouch it', As long as tinkers are allowed to earn their livings as tinkers and carry their pigskin tool-bag ('sowskin budget'), then I shall be able to account for myself and, when I am arrested on the charge of being a vagabond and am punished by being put in the stocks, I can assert ('avouch') that I am not a vagabond but a tinker (and show the arresting officer my leather bag to prove it and thus escape arrest) (Vagabonds and beggars, but not tinkers, were liable for arrest in Shakespeare's day)

'TIS, ''tis none of', she is in no way, IV iv 807

TO, about, I ii 270; see PASS, II ii 57; i.e. to speak of, IV iv 728; 'To her allowing husband', Towards her husband who complaisantly allows her to do so; 'To do', If I do, I ii 356; 'To do't, or no', If I kill Polixenes or I let him live, either; 'to yourself', see THEREABOUTS, I ii 379; 'bid . . . to's welcome', welcome these friends who are unknown to us

TOAZE, 'to toaze', in order to tease out (metaphor from the carding of wool)

TODS, see EVERY

TONGUE, i.e. praise, V i 106

TONGUELESS, 'One . . . tongueless . . . upon that', i.e. One good deed that goes unpraised means a thousand others which would otherwise follow it are never done

TOOTH, see PUGGING, IV iii 7

TOUCH'D, landed at, V i 139; 'as ever touch'd conjecture . . . sight only', as ever conjecture, which lacked only an actual sighting (of the crime), reached to

TOUCHES, fine details

TOYS, trivial things of no substance, III iii 39; trifling ornaments, IV iv 313

TRAFFIC, 'My traffic is . . . lesser linen', The merchandise ('traffic') in which I deal (i.e. 'steal') is sheets; when the kite is building its nest, look after your smaller pieces of linen (the kite was notorious for stealing small pieces of linen for nest-building; see KITE)

TRAIN, body of attendants, retinue; 'What train', What retinue is with him

TRAIN'D, (i) educated, (ii) (horticultural sense)

TRAITORLY, traitorous

TRANSPORTED, emotionally moved, V iii 69

TREACHERY, (i.e. the supposed plan to murder Leontes; see II i 47, II i 89)

TREMOR CORDIS, palpitation of the heart

TRESPASS, transgression, II ii 63

TRICK, toy, plaything, II i 51; characteristic form, expression, II iii 100

TRIFLES, 'makes but trifles . . . eyes', doesn't care what happens to his eyes (for I will scratch them with my nails)

TRIPP'D, i.e. sinned

TROLL-MY-DAMES, (i) a game played by 'trolling' balls through hoops on a board, (ii) (perhaps) loose-women (to 'troll' = to stroll about, to be passed round)

TROTH-PLIGHT, pledged to marry, V iii 151; the making of an engagement to marry (allusion to the fact that the making of an engagement to marry was sufficient in law for the couple to be recognised as fully married, although the Church felt that they would have sinned if they consummated their marriage before having had a church-wedding)

TRUE, see WHICH, I ii 284; honest, V ii 151

TRUMPERY, cheap wares

TRUMPET, trumpeter, herald (allusion to the fact that, on the field of battle, the trumpeter preceded the herald, who often wore red, and often bore angry messages)

TRUNK, (i) body (of mine), (ii) luggage-container (pun)

TRUNK-WORK, use of, concealment in, a trunk (see STAIR-WORK)

TRY, test, IV i 1

TUG . . . COME, contend for the future

TURN BACK, redound

TURTLE, turtledove (symbol of faithful love because turtledoves were believed to mate for life)

TWAIN, two

TWINN'D LAMBS, twin lambs, exactly like each other

TWO, 'One of these two . . . my life', i.e. One or other of two alternatives will be necessary: either you will have to renounce your resolve to marry me, or, if you persevere in your resolve, I shall have to change (or perhaps 'lose') my life

UNBRAIDED, new (probably 'not soiled')

UNBREECH'D, i.e. not yet old enough to wear breeches

UNCLASP'D, 'Unclasp'd my practice', Revealed my plot

UNCURRENT, see ENCOUNTER

UNDERTA'EN, undertaken (i.e. the murder of Leontes)

UNDISCOVER'D, unrevealed
UNDOES, 'undoes description . . . it', utterly defies description ('do' = describe)
UNFLEDG'D DAYS, days of infancy (when, like a fledgling bird, they did not yet possess flight-feathers)
UNFOLDS, unravels, reveals
UNGENTLE, ignoble, III iii 34
UNINTELLIGENT, unaware
UNMARRIED, see PRIMROSES
UNROLL'D, struck off the roll (of thieves)
UNROOSTED, driven from your perch
UNSPEAKABLE, unutterable, i.e. beyond reckoning, IV ii 39
UNSPHERE THE STARS, knock the stars from their normal courses (allusion to the Ptolemaic theory that the heavenly bodies revolved around the earth on a series of concentric crystalline spheres)
UNTHOUGHT-ON, 'But as th'unthought-on . . . do', But as the unexpected happening (i.e. Polixenes's intervention) is responsible for what we rashly are about to do
UNTHRIFTY . . . KNOWLEDGE, wasteful of a chance to increase our store of knowledge
UNTRIED, 'leave growth untried', the developments unexamined
UPON, see GROUND, II i 159; V iii 100
US, (often =) me (the royal plural)
USE (n.), 'is worth the use on't', has been well spent
US'D, treated (by me than was Hermione)
UTTER, see MEDDLER, IV iv 317

VALLEY, (perhaps) cleft of the chin, or groove in the upper lip
VAST, wide expanse (of land, sea, or time)
VENOM, poison
VERIER, see WAG
VERILY, In truth, indeed
VERY, see SOOTH, I ii 17; see SANCTITY, III iii 23; see BOND, IV iv 565
VESSEL, 'I never saw a vessel . . . becoming', I never saw someone so full of sorrow and who bore it so gracefully ('vessel' = (i) bearer, (ii) container, (iii) sailing vessel (the flowing robes and graceful movements of the woman are likened to the graceful sails and movement of a sailing vessel); 'becoming' = graceful)
VIALS, vessels
VICE, force, constrain (as by the use of a vice or clamp)
VILELY, meanly, wretchedly

VILLAIN, villainous (by saying such a thing), II i 80
VIRGINALLING, i.e. 'paddling' as if playing upon the virginals (a keyed musical instrument resembling a spinet), (see PADDLING)
VISAGE, 'By it own visage', i.e. Explicitly, plainly, in such a fashion that I can recognise it
VISIBLE, visibly, clearly
VISION, 'to vision so apparent', about something that can be so clearly seen
VOUCHSAF'D, designed, condescended
VULGARS, 'That vulgars . . . titles', To whom common people give the coarsest names

WAFTING, 'Wafting . . . contempt', Turning his eyes away and dropping his lip, contorting his mouth into an expression of great contempt
WAG, 'verier wag', more consummately mischievous boy
WAGGON, see PROSERPINA
WAITS, 'waits upon worn times', attends upon old age
WAKES, (village) festivals
WAKING, 'a waking', being awake, i.e. a real, not dreamed, experience
WANDER, see MOURN
WANT, lack, IV ii 12; be lacking, IV iv 586; 'wants but something to be', lacks a little something which would make him; 'wanted Less', i.e. were more lacking in ('Less' intensifies the idea of deficiency in 'wanted'); 'want'st', are lacking
WANTON (adj.), frisky, frolicsome, I ii 126; (v.), play, sport, II i 18
WARD, defensive posture (in fencing), I ii 33
WARDEN PIES, pies made with warden pears (a kind of cooking pear)
WARP, shrink, shrivel, change for the worse
WARRANT (v.), guarantee; 'I warrant you', I guarantee what I say is correct
WAS, which was, IV iv 359
WASH, (i.e. with his praising comparisons of IV iv 355ff.)
WATER, see SHED, III ii 190
WAT'RY STAR, i.e. the moon ('wat'ry' alludes to the connection between the moon and earthly tides; see NINE)
WAY, progress, V i 233; 'in a way', for a purpose (Florizel intends to marry Perdita), IV iv 33
WE, (often =) I (the royal plural)

WEAK-HING'D, i.e. flimsy, insecure, ill-founded

WEARING, garments

WEEDS, garments

WEEP (*see* III iii 32), III iii 51; 'weeping', *see* MARIGOLD, IV iv 106

WEIGH, *see* PRIZE (v.); 'not weighing . . . end', not properly considering, judging, the outcome (of my action)

WELKIN, i.e. sky-blue ('welkin' = sky)

WELL, i.e. in heaven, V i 30; 'well to live', well-to-do, prosperous (with pun on meaning 'living virtuously')

WERE, it would be, I ii 134; would be, I ii 318, IV iv 346, V i 29; *see* WHICH, I ii 283; 'wert', *see* LOOK, III ii 211

WESTWARD, in the west of the country (or 'West Country')

WHAT, *see* ALL, IV iv 685; 'What lady . . . lord', Less than any other lady – whoever she may be – loves her lord; 'What cheer', How are you feeling; 'What needs these hands', i.e. There is no need to lay hands on me; 'What with him', Who is with him

WHERE, Wherever, I ii 422; from where, IV iii 92; i.e. Of the man to whom, V i 213; 'Where were her life', i.e. (If I were a real tyrant, I would have ordered her execution by now); 'Where no priest . . . dust', (allusion to the fact that hanged criminals were buried under the gallows without a funeral service)

WHEREIN, 'Wherein our entertainment . . . loves', In that event our (poor) hospitality ('entertainment') would shame us were it not for the fact that we will be vindicated by our affection, which will make up for it (allusion to the Christian doctrine of salvation (or 'justification') by faith, i.e. that one's personal salvation depended primarily on the possession of religious faith, and not upon whether or not one performed good works)

WHEREOF, *see* CONJURE, I ii 401; 'Whereof the execution . . . non-performance', (probably) The carrying-out of which showed how wrong it would have been not to have done it (or 'Although the unperformed action was crying out to be done')

WHEREON, *see* OCCASION, I i 2

WHICH, *see* CLERK-LIKE EXPERIENC'D, I ii 932; *see* THING, II i 83; who, III ii 36, V ii 51; *see* MORE, III ii 58; 'which to reiterate . . . true', which, if one were to repeat it, the act of doing so, even if the accusation were well-founded, would be as sinful an act as (i) the sin of which you accuse her, (ii) your making such an accusation about her; 'which, if you . . . a truth like us', in respect of which, if you, either because you have really grown stupid or because you are cunningly pretending to be so ('seeming . . . skill'), cannot or will not perceive ('relish' = taste) something that is true as I can

WHILE, *see* WOE THE WHILE, III ii 169; 'the while', meanwhile, IV iv 48

WHILES, *see* COMFORT, I ii 197; while, V i 189

WHIP, *see* HINDER

WHISPER TO, secretly inform about; 'whisper him in your behalf', speak on your behalf to him in a whisper

WHISTLE OFF, release (term from falconry)

WHITSUN PASTORALS, (allusion to the May games, dances, and theatricals, customarily performed at Whitsuntide)

WHO, Whoever, III ii 40; i.e. My father, IV iii 24

WHOM, who, IV iv 353

WHOOBUB, hubbub, commotion

WHOOP, 'Whoop . . . man', (the refrain of a contemporary ribald ballad)

WHOSE, *see* FOUNDATION, I ii 429f.; 'whose daughter . . . parting with her', whose tears, when he parted from her, proclaimed her to be his daughter

WHY, '"Why to me"', 'Why is this insult offered to me'

WILD, rash, II i 182

WILDLY, madly, exuberantly

WINK, 'give mine . . . wink', close my enemy's eyes for ever; 'wink'd', closed my eyes, blinked

WISH'D, *see* SEIZ'D, V i 143

WIT, wisdom, good sense, II ii 52; ingenuity, IV iv 761

WITCHCRAFT, 'excellent witchcraft', i.e. at once bewitchingly beautiful and wickedly bewitching

WITH, by, V i 113, V ii 61, V iii 68

WITHAL, in addition, II i 153; with it, IV iv 669

WITHIN, i.e. as she is, II iii 26

WITHOUT, even without, IV iv 664

WITHOUT-DOOR FORM, exterior, external, appearance

WITNESS TO, witnessed (Time uses the present tense as he stands outside time), IV i 11

WOE THE WHILE, Alas (literally 'Who for the present time')

124

WOMAN-TIR'D, hen-pecked ('tire' = (in falconry) tear a piece of flesh with the beak)

WOMBS, contains within its womb

WOMEN, 'not women', i.e. that surely does not apply to women

WONT, accustomed

WORK, book, volume (i.e. 'son'), IV iv 21

WORSHIP, see BENCH'D, I ii 314

WORST, 'the worst', i.e. even if I were the least worthy, weakest, II iii 61

WORTH, valuable, V i 111

WORTHY, see FEEDING, IV iv 169; Worthy of, IV iv 427

WOTTING, If they know

WOULD, I wish that, I ii 99; I wish that I, II i 142; 'Would I were dead . . . already', May I die if it does not seem to me already (that it moves)

WROUGHT, moved

YEAST, foam

YELLOW, 'No yellow in't', Let there be no yellow (symbolic of jealousy) in it

YET, (often =) still; 'yet that . . . say', yet allow that Time himself says

YIELD, concede

YOK'D, 'yok'd . . . Best', rated as equally wicked as the name of the man (Judas) who betrayed Jesus

YOU, yourselves, I ii 179

YOUR, i.e. Florizel's, IV iv 570; 'Your worship had like . . . manner', Your honour would very likely have told us a lie (by claiming that salesmen often accuse soldiers to their face of lying) if you had not caught yourself in the act ('To be taken with the manner' = legal phrase for 'To be caught in the act of doing something unlawful')